CONFLICT
AND
ACCOMMODATION

CONTRIBUTIONS IN LABOR HISTORY

Class, Sex, and the Woman Worker
Milton Cantor and Bruce Laurie, editors

When Workers Fight: The Politics of Industrial Relations in the Progressive Era, 1898-1916
Bruno Ramirez

Domination, Legitimation, and Resistance: The Incorporation of the Nineteenth-Century English Working Class
Francis Hearn

The Knights of Labor in the South
Melton Alonza McLaurin

The Limits of Trade Union Militancy: The Lancashire Textile Workers, 1910-1914
Joseph L. White

Coal, Iron, and Slaves: Industrial Slavery in Maryland and Virginia, 1715-1865
Ronald L. Lewis

American Workingclass Culture: Explorations in American Labor and Social History
Milton Cantor, editor

Working-Class Community in Industrial America: Work, Leisure, and Struggle in Two Industrial Cities, 1880-1930
John T. Cumble

Organizing Dixie: Alabama Workers in the Industrial Era
Philip Taft, revised and edited by Gary M Fink

At the Point of Production: The Local History of the I.W.W.
Joseph R. Conlin, editor

CONFLICT AND ACCOMMODATION

COAL MINERS, STEEL WORKERS, AND SOCIALISM, 1890-1920

MICHAEL NASH

CONTRIBUTIONS IN LABOR HISTORY, NUMBER 11

GP

GREENWOOD PRESS
WESTPORT, CONNECTICUT • LONDON, ENGLAND

Library of Congress Cataloging in Publication Data

Nash, Michael, 1946-
    Conflict and accommodation.

    (Contributions in labor history, ISSN 0146-3608;
no. 11)
    Bibliography: p.
    Includes index.
    1. Coal-miners—miners—Pennsylvania—Political activity—His-
tory.   2. Iron and steel workers—Pennsylvania—Political
activity—History.   3. Elections—Pennsylvania—History.
4. Socialism—United States—History.   I. Title.   II. Series.
HD8079.P4N37   322'.2   81-6691
ISBN 0-313-22838-8 (lib. bdg.)   AACR2

Library of Congress Catalog Number: 81-6691
ISBN: 0-313-22838-8
ISSN: 0146-3608

First published in 1982

Greenwood Press
A division of Congressional Information Service, Inc.
88 Post Road West
Westport, Connecticut 06881

Printed in the United States of America

10 9 8 7 6 5 4 3 2 1

For my mother, Ruth, who was part of the struggle

Contents

Tables

Preface

What, if anything, will persuade workers to vote for socialism? This is the question that prompted me to analyze the political behavior of America's coal miners and steelworkers in the late nineteenth and early twentieth centuries. In the summer of 1971, when I first took up the question seriously, I hoped to do more than I have been able to do in this study, which relies heavily upon election analysis. Being young and ambitious beyond the possibilities, I sought to show that between 1870 and 1920, exploitation and violent labor-management conflict transformed the American working class into something resembling a class-conscious proletariat. After months of futile effort, I realized that writing a book of such scope was all but impossible. It would require a lifetime for a historian to penetrate the collective consciousness of a working class that was largely inarticulate.

As I pondered this problem, I began to consider how at least part of it might be illuminated by election analysis. Election statistics might well provide a clue to working-class consciousness. A vote for socialism might be seen as an expression of basic dissatisfaction with the capitalist system. A return by labor to either the Democratic or the Republican parties, on the other hand, would suggest that class consciousness had been dulled. An examination of Pennsylvania's precinct election returns for the 1870-1924 period soon revealed that violent strikes were followed by an upsurge in Populist and Socialist sentiment. Why did labor-management conflict affect voting behavior in this way, and why did support for Socialist (and Populist) parties dissipate almost as fast as it had developed? These questions became the focus of my concern.

In order to answer them, I examined the political behavior of America's coal miners and steelworkers. I decided to focus on these 600,000 men because, between 1900 and 1920, an era when the American Socialist party reached the peak of its strength, coal and steel were among the United States's largest industries. By 1900, steel, in value of product, was the largest. The 175,000 men who were employed in the nation's steel mills manufactured a product valued at $803,968,000. Similarly by 1900, the coal industry, which was rapidly growing in order to satisfy the nation's energy needs, had become the United States's sixth most productive industry. Here, 425,000 men (the largest number employed by any single industry) produced a product valued at $526 million.[1]

With some 600,000 men digging coal and manufacturing steel, identifiable coal and steel communities grew up. The election returns from these cities and towns help show how coal miners and steelworkers voted. Such data, together with more gathered from newspapers, union journals, government reports, and taped interviews, made it clear that violent strikes temporarily radicalized many coal miners and steelworkers. Before each of these strikes, the men (women were not yet voting) usually voted for whatever Democratic or Republican politicians bothered to campaign as friends of the working class. However, during strikes, especially when the state militia or the federal army sided with the bosses by beating up strikers and supporting strikebreakers, workers had good reason to turn to radical third parties. Each blow they received helped teach them much about the relationship between the state and capitalism. So it was that violent class conflict made the Socialist message meaningful. Karl Marx appears to have been correct, at least to this degree, when he predicted that class conflict would radicalize the working class.

Unfortunately for the Socialists, however, the history of modern industrial society has not been a history of class struggles. On the contrary, if modern American history has a significant theme, it is the success of the capitalists in blunting the class struggle that Socialists hoped would radicalize the working class. Instead of constant conflict leading to a revolutionary synthesis, a dialectic of conflict and accommodation has been characteristic of American labor history. Time and again when class struggle threatened to radicalize workers, the captains of industry responded by raising wages, introducing welfare capitalism, or recognizing their employees' trade unions. In these ways, they cut the ground out from under the Socialists. How this dialectic worked itself out between 1890 and 1920 in the coal and steel industries is my concern.

This book has benefited enormously from the help of Charles Forcey. He spent months with various versions of the manuscript, rewriting most sections of it line by line. For his patience and instruction in the writing of history, I will always be indebted. Melvyn Dubofsky was also wonderfully helpful. He spent many hours with me and was a constant source of fruitful ideas.

I would like to thank James Axelrod of Berea College. His taped interviews with retired West Virginia coal miners provided much of the material for chapter 6. Jim not only made his tapes available to me but was a gracious host when I descended upon him for ten days during October 1972.

Every researcher owes a debt to librarians and archivists. This study benefited from the splendid assistance provided by the staffs from the National Archives and the State Historical Society of Wisconsin. I am grateful for the cooperation I received from the people who work at the manuscript divisions of the New York Public Library, Catholic University Library, Pennsylvania State University Library, Duke University Library, and Cornell University's M. P. Catherwood Library. I would like to thank Janet Brown of the SUNY-Binghamton Library for her help in locating most of the obscure newspapers used in this book. I am also very grateful to Emily Taft Douglas for giving me permission to use some of the real wage tables that were originally constructed by her late husband, Paul Douglas, for his book *Real Wages in the United States, 1890-1926* (Boston: Houghton Mifflin, 1930). Finally, I would like to thank my wife, Jeanne, whose help and encouragement is far greater than she realizes.

Note

1. U.S. Bureau of the Census, *Abstract of the Twelfth Census of the United States, 1900* (Washington, D.C.: Government Printing Office, 1904), pp. 322-426.

Introduction

Why, during the early years of the twentieth century, was the United States the only industrialized nation in the world without a powerful Socialist movement? Traditionally, historians have answered this question by arguing that socialism was irrelevant in the United States because America was, among other things, a "land of opportunity." Since upwardly mobile American workers had (compared to the rest of the world) a relatively high standard of living, they naturally chose to become aspiring capitalists, not revolutionaries. In 1948, for example, Richard Hofstadter's *American Political Tradition* unequivocally asserted:

In material power and productivity the United States has been a flourishing success. Societies that are in such good working order have a mute organic consistency. They do not foster ideas that are hostile to their fundamental working arrangement.[1]

Hofstadter was stating strongly a thesis that became basic to much of his later work, though the book cited actually contradicted much of it. This consensus thesis has intrigued scholars for a generation; only recently has it been subjected to critical reevaluation. Stephan Thernstrom among others has raised serious questions about the rags-to-riches myth by demonstrating that social mobility was, in fact, limited in nineteenth-century America. Workers rarely rose into the ranks of the middle and upper classes.[2] Moreover, between 1890 and 1910, while the U.S. economy, in Walt W. Rostow's phrase, "drove toward maturity," applying the "range of modern technology to its resources," control of industry became concentrated in fewer and fewer hands. By the end of this period, 1 percent of the nation's manufacturing firms were producing 44 percent of all manufactured goods.[3] The men and women who were employed by these firms worked ten or twelve hours a day for subsistence wages.

During these years it appeared to many that the American labor force was not receiving a fair share of the nation's wealth. Between 1890 and 1910, while the U.S. annual net national product increased from $13.1 billion to $35.6 billion (some 290 percent), average real wages rose by only 2 percent.[4] Wages could be held down because working-class efforts at unionization were largely frustrated. In 1910, only 10 percent of the American labor force was organized.[5] When trade unions struck to demand recognition, capitalists usually responded by summoning the state militia or the army to escort strikebreakers through the picket lines. As a result, bloody clashes, like the ones that took place at Homestead (1892), Pullman (1894), Cripple Creek (1904), and Ludlow (1914), occurred with disturbing frequency.

The United States was not an organically unified society in 1900. The American consensus that scholars such as Richard Hofstadter, Louis Hartz, and Daniel Boorstin have celebrated so eloquently was forged during a half-century of class struggle. For a while, it appeared as if violence and the class consciousness that went with it might permanently fracture the American social fabric. And, in fact, consensus did not supersede conflict until certain influential capitalists began to see that it was necessary for them to seek an accommodation with their employees. Fearing that a polarization of society would lead to a Socialist revolution, some industrialists—Mark Hanna of Hanna Coal and Iron and William McKinley's 1896 campaign manager was one—concluded that they had no choice but to promote harmony between labor and capital. Once the group around Hanna recognized labor as an interest group with a legitimate claim upon society's wealth, the American social fabric lost what many Socialists of the time regarded as hopeful friability. By the mid-twentieth century, after the New Deal with its Wagner Act and the organization of the Congress of Industrial Organizations, the United States became a relatively conflict-free society. Almost forty years after Hanna's death, his corporate vision triumphed over that of such Socialist leaders as Eugene Debs.

The failure of socialism is my major theme here. Election returns from coal miners and steelworkers provide a significant clue. Only recently social historians have begun to recognize the value of quantitative election analysis. Richard Jensen and Paul Kleppner, for example, have made significant efforts in this area. In their studies of late-nineteenth-century midwestern voting behavior, they discovered that religious and ethnic variables usually took precedence over economic factors in determining political affiliation. Being consensus historians, they reasoned from these data that the Democratic and Republican parties were "responsive coalitions," sensitive to the "needs and aspirations" of the voters.[6]

This conclusion, however, may well fail to survive a closer look at the data. The electorate may not have divided along class lines because workers and farmers had few, if any, economic reasons for voting for either of the major political parties. After all, what could they have realistically expected from men like Grover Cleveland and William McKinley beyond minor squabbles as to how high the tariff should be? Paul Kleppner points out, for instance, that in many working-class districts, less than 40 percent of the eligible voters usually went to the polls. There is good reason to suspect that some of these men were making a political statement by their absence. The evidence suggests that many would have cast ballots for the Populist or Socialist parties if these organizations had been able to reach them. Kleppner and Jensen themselves show, for another example, that during the 1894 coal strike, when the leadership of the United Mine Workers actively campaigned for the Populist party, populism made an impact in many coal towns. Kleppner claims that this shift to populism did not "connote an ideological agreement" with the Populists' radical critique of American society. Instead, it represented a negative reaction to the Democratic party's failure to present a program to combat the depression. This statement cannot be accepted at face value. On the contrary, the election of 1894 demonstrated that violent strikes, which forced the class issue into the political arena, could polarize the electorate along class lines.[7]

Between 1894 and 1916 violent class conflict regularly polarized America's steel and coal communities. To see such polarization in meaningful context, though, requires some consideration of the era's Socialist movement, especially the ambivalence of the party's response to violence. The first chapter opens the way to our question. Chapter 2 focuses on the economic structure of the industries. Reasons why trade unionism succeeded in coal but failed in steel are explored. Chapter 3 shows how strikes, which resulted in the unionization of the coal industry, also temporarily radicalized the miners. But chapter 4 carries the analysis further to suggest why the triumph of trade unionism, despite such radicalism, led to the failure of socialism. Chapter 5 contrasts the political behavior of the unionized coal miners with that of the nonunion steelworkers, who by 1911 were voting for socialism in large numbers. Finally, chapter 6 provides a closing for the theme by dealing with two nonunion coalfields: Westmoreland County, Pennsylvania (1910-1922), and Kanawha County, West Virginia (1912-1913). The battles that took place in these areas were bloody. Even a grueling year of class struggle, however, was not enough to radicalize permanently the West Virginia coal miners. The shooting stopped. The United Mine Workers gained recognition. Most of the Socialists' votes among the miners soon returned to the Democratic and Republican parties. Only the Westmoreland County miners, whose strike ended in abject defeat, continued voting Socialist until the United States entered World War I in 1917.

"What might have been?" is a question too little asked in academe. This essay asks it. Could the U.S. political economy have evolved differently? To ask and answer the question helps us understand how the development of modern corporate capitalism foreclosed a Socialist alternative.

Notes

1. Richard Hofstadter, *The American Political Tradition* (New York: Alfred A. Knopf, 1948), p. viii; *see also* Daniel Bell, *Marxian Socialism in the United States* (Princeton: Princeton University Press, 1957), and Louis Hartz, *The Liberal Tradition in America* (New York: Harcourt Brace and World, 1966).

2. Stephan Thernstrom, *Poverty and Progress* (Cambridge: Harvard University Press, 1964); *see also* David Brody, *Steel Workers in America: The Non-Union Era* (Cambridge: Harvard University Press, 1960); Victor Greene, *The Slavic Community on Strike* (Notre Dame: Notre Dame University Press, 1968); Herbert Gutman, "Work, Culture and Society in Industrializing America, 1815-1919," *American Historical Review* 78 (June 1973):531-89; and Stephan Thernstrom, *The Other Bostonians: Poverty and Progress in the Metropolis* (Cambridge: Harvard University Press, 1973).

3. The phrase "drive toward maturity" was taken from W. W. Rostow, *The Stages of Economic Growth* (Cambridge: Cambridge University Press, 1960), p. 58. According to Rostow, the U.S. economy drove toward maturity between 1900 and 1920. The statistics on concentration of industry were taken from David Shannon, *Twentieth Century America* (Chicago: Rand McNally, 1963), pp. 57-58.

4. U.S. Bureau of the Census, *Historical Statistics of the United States, Colonial Times to 1957* (Washington, D.C.: Government Printing Office, 1960). Between 1890 and 1910 average money wages increased by 22 percent from $486 to $630 a year, but the cost of living rose by 20 percent. Paul Douglas, *Real Wages in the United States, 1890-1926* (Boston: Houghton Mifflin, 1930), pp. 52-64.

5. U.S. Bureau of the Census, *Historical Statistics,* pp. 97-98.

6. Richard Jensen, *The Winning of the Midwest: Social and Political Conflict, 1888-1896* (Chicago: University of Chicago Press, 1971); Paul Kleppner, *The Cross of Culture: A Social Analysis of Midwestern Politics, 1850-1900* (New York: The Free Press, 1970); and Paul Kleppner, *The Third Electoral System, 1853-1892* (Chapel Hill: University of North Carolina Press, 1979).

7. Kleppner, *Cross of Culture,* p. 260; for a devastating review of Kleppner's work, *see* James R. Green, "Behavioralism and Class Analysis: A Review Essay on Methodology and Ideology," *Labor History* 13 (Winter 1972):89-106.

CONFLICT
AND
ACCOMMODATION

The Socialists
and the Revolution
<u>CHAPTER</u> 1

The German-born Karl Marx, coauthor of the *Communist Manifesto* and author of *Das Kapital,* is the central figure in the history of socialism. In these writings, he constructed a social theory that he claimed explained not only how the capitalist system evolved but also proved scientifically that capitalism was inherently self-destructive. Marx's model for social change was so appealing to European and American radicals that by the late nineteenth century it had become the creed of the modern Socialist movement.

The optimistic Marx of the mid-nineteenth century asserted that as the bourgeois class developed, it would call another class into being, its dialectical antithesis, the proletariat. As more and more production was concentrated into factories, the laboring class would become larger and hence stronger. In addition, as competitive conditions grew more intense, Marx believed that the bourgeoisie would devour each other until the means of production became concentrated in a very few hands. In the end, Marx saw the proletarianized mass expropriating the mines and factories from a powerful and yet totally vulnerable bourgeoisie.[1]

As early as 1848, when the *Communist Manifesto* was published, Marx observed that "society as a whole [was] splitting into two hostile camps, into two great classes, directly facing each other: bourgeoisie and proletariat."² He saw intense class conflict as inevitably resulting from this social division. "Modern industry has converted the little workshop of the patriarchal master into the great factory of the industrial capitalist," declared the *Communist Manifesto:*

Masses of laborers, crowded into factories, are organized like soldiers. Not only are they slaves of the bourgeois class, and the bourgeois state; they are daily and hourly enslaved by the machine, by the overlooker, and above all by the individual manufacturer himself. The more openly this despotism proclaims gain to be its aim, the more petty, the more hateful, the more embittering it is.³

Marx knew, or so he thought, how a maturing capitalism would destroy itself. Machines, by displacing skilled artisans and throwing millions of men and women out of work, would create a "reserve army" of unemployed laborers. With workers competing for scarce jobs, capitalists would pay merely subsistence wages, but such would be their fatal mistake. With wages falling and unemployment increasing, capitalism's sophisticated machinery would produce more goods than an impoverished working class could purchase. Consequently, in industrial societies, depressions, crises caused by overproduction, were inevitble. Marx thought that capitalism would break down under the weight of these crises.⁴

Marx reasoned that poverty and increasingly intense exploitation would force the workers to organize in order to defend themselves. The working class would pass through various stages of development in its struggle with the bourgeoisie. At first, its members would fight individually, then in a single factory make common cause. Later the workers of a trade would combine. At this stage, the bosses would feel constrained to unite. The resultant class struggle, so Marx thought, would transform the working class from a "class in itself" into a "class for itself." The class-conscious men and women would then seize both the state and the means of production.⁵

During the late nineteenth and early twentieth centuries, there seemed to be a possibility that Marx's predictions would come true. As the pace of industrialization quickened, Marxist Social Democratic parties, organized in most Western European nations during the 1870s, steadily increased in strength. According to Carl Schorske, a leading historian of German socialism, there was a high correlation between "the intensity of the class struggle and political radicalism," as the Socialists usually found striking workers to be particularly responsive to their appeals.[6] By 1914, 2.2 million Socialists, joined by 6.4 million nonregistered Socialists, were sending 448 deputies to Europe's parliaments.[7]

By 1914, however, the movement bore little resemblance to that which Karl Marx had known. As Socialist parties grew in strength and influence, they lost much of their revolutionary zeal. By the turn of the century, they had developed an elaborate bureaucratic structure. Their assets ran into the millions. Each party controlled a vast network of newspapers and publishing houses, and each administered building societies, welfare funds, and producer and consumer cooperatives. Wielding considerable power and influence, party officials began to develop vested interests and conservative temperaments. The stronger the movement became, the more it stood to lose in any violent battle for state power. Trade unionists, who achieved positions of power within the movement because they provided the Socialists with access to the rank-and-file workers, grew particularly cautious, especially when successful in negotiating collective-bargaining agreements. These men could no longer be uncompromisingly committed to the vigorous pursuit of the class struggle since their contracts permitted strikes or other demonstrations of labor power only under specified conditions.[8]

An alternative to orthodox Marxism came from the self-made scholar, Eduard Bernstein, who, while in exile in England during the 1880s and 1890s, had begun to subject Marxism to a critical reevaluation or revision. Bernstein's observations led him to conclude that capitalism had a capacity for adjustment that would minimize the likelihood and impact of severe economic crises. New credit mechanisms, market controls, cartels, and an imperialist control of a world market appeared to have stabilized capitalism. Bernstein concluded that with wages steadily rising, society would not polarize into two hostile camps. Nor did the middle class and its small businessmen appear to be disappearing. Their numbers were in fact steadily increasing. If Socialists hoped to achieve power, they would have to develop programs designed to appeal to bourgeois as well as proletarian groups. Bernstein warned that if the party ever wanted to gain such support it had to "emancipate itself from the revolutionary phraseology" and become a "democratic socialist party of reform."[9]

In their effort to counter Bernstein's thesis, Marxists would often point to the United States, arguing that the land of the trust was going to give birth to the socialist revolution. In *European Socialists and the American Promised Land,* R. Laurence Moore has shown that many radicals viewed the appearance of trusts on the American scene as a confirmation of Marxian economic theory. In 1903, Paul Lafargue, Karl Marx's French son-in-law, declared that "if Karl Marx's materialistic theory of history had a need of a new and dazzling confirmation, the trusts would furnish it."[10] W. C. Owens of the British Social Democratic Federation similarly concluded that American capitalists "by the introduction of the 'trust' [were] . . . crushing out and turning into revolutionaries the whole previously conservative middle class."[11]

The dominant faction within the Socialist party of America, led by the austere Teutonic schoolteacher, Victor Berger, did not agree with this analysis. As chairman of the party's National Executive Committee, Berger echoed Bernstein's criticism of Marxists who failed "to recognize the evolutionary nature of social change." He argued that socialism would not be inaugurated after a catastrophic revolution but would slowly evolve as capitalism reformed itself.[12] American revisionists believed that such things as legal limitations on dividends from public service corporations and public control of police departments and post offices were "examples of real socialism."[13] To them, campaigning for socialism meant fighting for municipal ownership of streetcars and public utilities.[14]

American right-wing Socialists shared German revisionist aversions to socialism as an exclusively proletarian movement.

They warned that a radical movement that looked for support only among the working class would be doomed to failure, if only because most workers were not revolutionary. Victor Berger thought the masses "stupid, indolent, philistines" to whom social progress could not be entrusted. Only the intellectuals, he maintained, could persuade Americans to establish a Socialist society.[15] Like other right wingers, he warned that if intellectuals did not guide the Socialist movement "ignorant and desperate workers" would seek socialism through "force and bloodshed." Berger preached to all capitalists who might listen that socialism was the only way to avoid class warfare. He and his followers took it upon themselves to work for "class understanding" through the "development of mutual class respect." They wanted the party to work for reform and stop using "stupid phrases and senseless catchwords like social revolution."[16]

With such emphasis on reform, Berger often seemed to lose sight of the distinction between progressivism and socialism. In fact, many of the reforms he advocated such as workers' compensation and the eight-hour day were similar to those being campaigned for by progressive Republicans and Democrats who were often financed and supported by industrialists like George Perkins of the United States Steel Corporation and Mark Hanna of Hanna Coal and Iron, men who saw reform as an antidote for socialism.

Socialists like Victor Berger were confused by such tactics. Instead of trying to expose the real motives of the progressive capitalists, they accused Theodore Roosevelt and the Progressive party of stealing their platform. Yet the revisionists never asked themselves, at least in public, whether a platform that could be so easily stolen by a capitalist party was in fact Socialist.[17] At any rate, with many of the key planks of the Socialist party's program expropriated, workers had very little reason to vote for the Socialists. Instead in 1912, large numbers of them voted for the supposedly radical Progressive party.[18] Thus Eugene Debs, running on the Socialists' line, received a mere 6 percent of the vote, while Theodore Roosevelt got more than 30 percent.

For a long time Marxist revolutionaries had been predicting

that the triumph of revisionism would lead to such a disaster. Men like William Haywood, the Colorado silver miner and organizer for the Industrial Workers of the World (IWW), who had come to socialism as a result of his experiences as an industrial unionist, were disgusted by Berger's moderation. Haywood, whose ideas were an amalgamation of Marxism and French syndicalism, believed that social change could be brought about only by class struggle. He argued that the only way to make the working class revolutionary was by "exercising its members in constant struggle against the capitalists in the mines, factories, and other places of work."[19] Haywood saw such conflict leading to a general strike and revolution. Unlike European syndicalists, however, Haywood, who ran for governor of Colorado in 1906, urged "every workman to use the ballot at every opportunity."[20] He did not believe that such political action would produce working-class emancipation, but he hoped that the proletariat might capture some governmental offices and thus protect itself against the power of the state.

Haywood's ideology was anathema to Victor Berger. Consequently, by 1912, the revisionists began accusing him of advocating "violence and lawbreaking." In 1913, after months of bitter debate, Big Bill Haywood was recalled from the Socialist party's National Executive Committee for allegedly advocating industrial sabotage.

The departure of Haywood did not leave the Marxists without a party spokesman. Eugene Debs, a four-time presidential candidate and also founding member of the IWW, was as critical of revisionism as Haywood was. Debs's disagreements with Haywood were largely over tactics. While the IWW leader believed that the working class would emancipate itself on the barricades, Debs saw liberation taking place at the polls. Debs believed that the Marxian model was applicable to the American experience. He charged the revisionists with abandoning their faith in revolutionary socialism in order to woo voters and elect candidates to office. The Socialist party's perennial presidential candidate was appalled by the way Berger diluted the party's program in order to appeal to the middle class. He argued that the party had to campaign unequivocally for the nationalization of the means of production.[21] Socialists should have nothing to do with reform movements, which were at best products of the quarrels "between big and little capital" as to "who should have the privilege of robbing the working class." What Debs and other radicals wanted was involvement in labor's struggles in order to gain the confidence of the working class.[22]

Debs argued that if Socialists campaigned as Marxists, the party would succeed in convincing the working class to vote to abolish capitalism. He claimed that since the "general tendency of capitalist production [was] . . . not to raise, but to sink the average standard of wages," workers, who were forced to fight constantly against the "encroachments of capital," would eventually see that they had to vote to abolish the wage system.[23]

In line with their belief that Bernstein's economic analysis was fallacious, left-wing Socialists tended to underestimate the resiliency of the capitalist system and the resourcefulness of the capitalist class. Capitalists, in fact, were not oblivious to the threat that class struggle presented to their hegemony. By 1900 men like Mark Hanna, Andrew Carnegie, Elbert H. Gary, and George Perkins had concluded that "nothing [was] . . . more pressing than finding a method of adjusting the differences between labor and capital."[24] As if to set up a model for a corporate society, these men organized the tripartite National Civic Federation, (NCF). It enlisted representatives of the business community, the public, and labor leaders like Samuel Gompers and United Mine Workers president John Mitchell. The NCF hoped to be able to persuade the working class to settle its differences with capital by conciliation and arbitration.[25] As the $8,000 a year head of the NCF's trade agreements department, John Mitchell became responsible for the day-to-day implementation of this policy.

Hanna, Perkins, and Gary were constantly debating the relative merits of various approaches for undercutting the Socialists. Gary argued that if capitalists paid their employees well and paternalistically looked after their welfare, they could "cultivate a feeling of friendship," which would discourage their employees from turning to either trade unionism or socialism. Hanna, on the other hand, was not opposed to organized labor.

He recognized that the conservative craft unionism of the AFL was a "perfect antidote for Socialism." He saw "conservative, respectable trade unions" as providing the capitalists with a "ready and willing ally in the fight against Socialism."[26]

Left-wing socialists were very much aware of the challenge of the NCF. Like Mark Hanna, they knew that if the American working class became wedded to the AFL's conservative policy of avoiding strikes at all costs, class conflict would be blunted and the Socialist party crippled. Debs and Haywood could not understand how Victor Berger could defend Gompers's and Mitchell's class collaborationist tactics. When Berger argued that the Socialist party should try to convert the AFL to socialism, Debs responded by claiming that he could better spend his time "spraying a cess pool with attar of roses."[27]

Confronted with the NCF, the IWW maintained that labor should refuse to sign contracts with capitalists. Hoping for perpetual class warfare, the IWW claimed that such agreements were "no more binding than the title deed to a negro slave."[28] With such a policy, however, the Wobblies, as IWW members were called, could only offer a seemingly endless struggle. Being good Marxists, they hoped that such a struggle would radicalize the working class. But would the hoped-for general strike and revolution occur before exhaustion, starvation, or the promise of increased wages forced labor to seek an accommodation with capitalism?

NOTES

1. Karl Marx and Frederick Engels, "The Manifesto of the Communist Party," in Lewis Feuer, ed., *Marx and Engels: Basic Writings on Politics and Philosophy* (New York: Anchor Books, 1959), pp. 3-52.

2. Ibid., p. 8.

3. Ibid., p. 13.

4. Ibid., pp. 20-22.

5. Ibid., p. 15; Irving Zeitlin, *Marxism: A Re-Examination* (Princeton: Princeton University Press, 1967), p. 57.

6. Carl Schorske, *German Social Democracy, 1905-1917* (Cambridge: Harvard University Press, 1955), p. 90.

7. Country	Number of Members	Number of Votes in Last Election before 1914	Number of Socialist Deputies	Total Number of Deputies
Austria	145,000	1,000,000 (1911)	82	516
Belgium		600,000 (1912)	39	185
Denmark	25,000	107,365 (1913)	32	240
France	90,700	1,379,860 (1914)	101	602
Germany	1,851,905	4,250,329 (1912)	110	397
Great Britain	60,000[a]	370,802 (1910)	42	670
Italy	40,000	338,865 (1909)	42	508

[a]Figure does not include 1,501,092 members of trade unions affiliated with the Labour party.
Source: Julius Braunthal, *History of the International* (New York: Praeger, 1967), I 1:351; Merle Fainsod, *International Socialism and the World War* (Cambridge: Harvard University Press, 1935), p. 40; J. Bruce Glasier, *Socialist Yearbook* (London: National Labour Press, 1913), pp. 5-98.

8. Schorske, *German Social Democracy,* p. 270; G. D. H. Cole, *The Second International* (London: Macmillan, 1956).

9. Peter Gay, *The Dilemma of Democratic Socialism: Eduard Bernstein's Challenge to Marx* (New York: Columbia University Press, 1950).

10. R. Laurence Moore, *European Socialists and the American Promised Land* (New York: Oxford University Press, 1970), p. 84.

11. Ibid., p. 91.

12. Victor Berger, "How It Will Probably Come," *Social Democratic Herald,* January 4, 1902.

13. Berger often referred to "police department socialism." *See Social Democratic Herald,* January 19, 1901, April 24, 1902.

14. Ibid.

15. Victor Berger, "Moving by the Light of Reason," *Social Democratic Herald,* April 15, 1905; Victor Berger, "Classes in Free America," *Social Democratic Herald,* January 13, 1906.

16. Victor Berger, "A Word to the Rich," *Social Democratic Herald,* August 8, 1903.

17. Ibid.; W. J. Ghent, in the *Social Democratic Herald,* September 28, 1912; Ira Kipnis, *The American Socialist Movement, 1897-1912* (New York: Columbia University Press, 1952), p. 216.

18. Ralph Easley, NCF executive secretary, estimated that Theodore

Roosevelt's candidacy cost the Socialist party 300,000 votes. Ralph Easley to Theodore Roosevelt, November 18, 1912, National Civic Federation Papers, New York Public Library.

19. On Haywood, *see* Joseph Conlin, *Big Bill Haywood and the Radical Union Movement* (Syracuse: Syracuse University Press, 1969); Melvyn Dubofsky, *We Shall Be All: A History of the Industrial Workers of the World* (Chicago: Quadrangle, 1969); Haywood quoted in the *Newcastle Free Press,* October 12, 1909.

20. Haywood quoted in the *Newcastle Free Press,* October 19, 1909.

21. Debs quoted in Kipnis, *American Socialist Movement,* p. 407.

22. Eugene Debs, "This Is Our Year," *International Socialist Review* (July 1912); Eugene Debs, "Danger Ahead," *International Socialist Review* (January 1911):414-16.

23. Eugene Debs, "Unionism and Socialism," in Arthur Schlesinger, Jr., *Writings and Speeches of Eugene V. Debs* (New York: Hermitage Press, 1948), pp. 95-125.

24. Gary and Perkins were two of J. P. Morgan's most prominent partners. When the billion-dollar United States Steel Corporation was organized in 1901, Gary was named chairman of the executive board, and Perkins became chairman of the Finance committee.

25. Marcus A. Hanna, in the *National Civic Federation Monthly Review* (June 1902); the standard work on the NCF is James Weinstein, *The Corporate Ideal in the Liberal State* (Boston: Beacon Press, 1968).

26. E. H. Gary speech given on May 4, 1911, before the board of directors of the United States Steel Corporation. The text is in "Addresses and Speeches of E. H. Gary," unpublished manuscript, New York Public Library; Marcus Alonzo Hanna, "Industrial Conciliation and Arbitration," *Annals of the American Academy of Political and Social Sciences* 40 (December 1902):28-29.

27. Debs quoted in *Chicago Socialist,* December 23, 1908.

28. Dubofsky, *We Shall Be All,* p. 165. All quotations where "Negro" has not been capitalized have been left as is without [*sic*].

Coal and Steel During Prosperity and Depression, 1880-1900

CHAPTER 2

Marxists who lived during the 1890s, a decade that combined tremendous economic growth with a major depression, might very well have concluded that the American capitalist system was about to break down. The economy seemed right on the road Karl Marx had predicted. Industrial capital increased by more than 50 percent from $6.525 billion to $9.814 billion. Yet seeming to conform to Marx's predictions, the United States was gripped by its worst depression ever.[1] In the spring of 1893, a few months after President Benjamin Harrison told Congress that "there has never been a time in our history when work was so abundant or when wages were so high," the country was hit by a paralyzing financial panic.[2] By the winter of 1893-1894, the economy was producing at only 75 percent of capacity. Two and one-half million Americans, 20 percent of the nation's labor force, were unemployed. The unemployment picture did not improve until 1895, and then only briefly; the next year the depression worsened. It was 1898 before recovery became fully apparent. Even as late as 1900, the average worker's real annual wage was 10 percent lower than it had been in 1893.[3]

Despite the depression, the industrial revolution accelerated. In the 1880s, American factories were largely devoted to the processing of products of the farm and forest. By 1900, the products of the nation's mines had become industry's most important raw material. In 1890, the United States's three most important industries (by value of their products) were processed meat, flour and grains, and timber products. By 1900, iron and steel had become the nation's leading industry. During the 1890s its production more than doubled from 4,277,000 gross tons to 10,188,000 gross tons. Coal mining moved up from tenth to sixth place, its production increasing by more than 50 percent from 157,870,000 tons to 269,684,027 tons.[4]

Until the mid-1880s, America's iron and steel mills were by later standards quite primitive. Procedures were largely manual. The skilled puddler, who removed carbon from pig iron by bringing it, in its molten state, into contact with the air, was a central figure. Only after many years could he learn how to stir molten pig iron in such a way as to produce quality wrought iron. Rollers, catchers, and roughers, who took the red-hot wrought iron and hammered it into malleable bar iron, were also highly skilled.[5]

Men with such essential skills met little resistance when in 1876 they organized the Amalgamation Association of Iron and Steel Workers. The new union, however, was soon tested by the strike wave that marked the mid-1870s. In 1876, work stoppages gripped much of the Pittsburgh district. The next year saw thousands of steelworkers walking off their jobs in sympathy with the striking railroad workers. The 1877 strike has been characterized as the most violent in American labor history, and Pennsylvania was the scene of much of the bloodshed.[6]

The Amalgamated Association, however, quickly recovered from these strikes and continued to gain in strength. By the mid-1880s it had 24,000 dues-paying members. By 1891, 70 percent of the skilled iron workers and steelworkers were members. The union's bylaws excluded from membership unskilled steelworkers, who then made up only 20 percent of the industry's labor force.[7] The union leadership, who had seen the Amalgamated succeed in establishing a virtual closed shop in most of the mills in the Pittsburgh district, did not believe that the strength of their organization would be jeopardized by the exclusion of the unskilled worker.[8]

A closed shop meant high wages for union members. Wages were based on the price of iron and steel. The union had enough power to control output, and in frequently glutted markets this meant that it could control wages. As a consequence, through most of the 1880s, unionized steelworkers were among the best-paid men in the United States. Most American workers earned about $300 a year. The skilled iron workers and steelworkers often earned three times that much. Even unskilled men who were not members of the union earned as much as $400 a year. Union contracts, in order to protect the price of hard-won skills, mandated that these men be paid wages that averaged 40 percent of those of skilled workers.[9] Thus few iron workers and steelworkers, skilled or unskilled, complained about their wages. "I cannot speak too highly of the method of paying at the mills," a Pittsburgh puddler declared. "Where I am employed, thanks to the Amalgamated Association, . . . I receive fair wages."[10]

Nor, thanks to the union, were working conditions too bad. Fifty-eight pages of footnotes in the union contract regulated such conditions together with the quality and quantity of iron and steel produced in the mills. Management had to consult the union before it could introduce technical or procedural innovations, and the Amalgamated often vetoed plans designed to increase efficiency and production.[11]

Union control over working conditions and productivity created many problems for management. The workers probably could have produced their daily quota of iron or steel in eight hours, yet many resisted any management effort to introduce the eight-hour day. The men, having long arranged their starting and quitting time themselves, feared that a standardized day would lead to a three-shift system, which would make it impossible for them to continue to work at their accustomed pace. Their usual day ran from nine to twelve hours. On such a schedule, they could leave the mill for a midday beer at the local tavern or for other diversions and errands of varying duration. Beer and liquor undoubtedly interfered with the efficient operation of the mills. Not only management but the union leadership, therefore, came to be temperance advocates. The *National Labor Tribune,* the Amalgamated Association's official publication, constantly and unsuccessfully pleaded with the men not to leave the mills for the taverns, arguing that intoxicated men endangered the safety of their sober brethren.[12]

Controversy about noontime saloon trips suggested that few steelworkers, even as late as the 1880s, had internalized the Protestant ethic. Still, both management and the union leadership continued to try to rationalize the industry. In January of each year they determined what the average price of iron and steel had been during the past twelve months and agreed upon a scale of wages. The workers, whatever their disagreements on the liquor issue, had confidence in the system, which, by such a calculation, included their relaxations. They rarely went out on strike and often even accepted wage reductions with good grace. One worker in the early 1880s summed up the aura of trust:

The workmen at our mills are members of the Amalgamated Association of Iron and Steel Workers and a committee of workmen and managers consult and arrange the wages on the first of each year. The scale or schedule agreed upon is signed by both parties and as a result we have no trouble. We have just accepted a reduction of 13 percent all around and last year we accepted a reduction of 15 percent.[13]

In somewhat the same spirit, management behaved reasonably when it met with the union leadership at the annual joint conference. The mill owners wanted to avoid unnecessary conflicts with a wealthy union of the skilled committed to paying strike benefits.[14] As long as skilled workers were in short supply, normal for a relatively new and rapidly expanding industry, management dared not challenge the union's power.

By the mid-1880s, however, technological change began to undermine the position of the skilled workers. The open hearth furnace, perfected during this decade, heated iron far beyond its melting point, making it possible to burn off carbon from pig iron without puddling. By 1900, few of the once-proud and essential puddlers were working in the steel mills of the Pittsburgh district.[15] Nor were the puddlers alone. As the mills modernized and steel replaced wrought iron, thousands of catchers, rollers, and roughers became superfluous. Machine tenders took the place of skilled workers. In 1881, 80 percent of America's iron workers and steelworkers were classified as skilled; by 1891, only 60 percent of them were so classified. By the turn of the century, unskilled workers outnumbered the skilled.[16] Two decades had dramatically changed a situation where the Amalgamated could virtually ignore the unskilled steelworkers.

So rapid a change resulted in large part from the cut-throat competition, characteristic of the iron and steel industry at the time. Steel magnates who hoped to survive had to adopt innovations quickly. They were desperate to reduce costs to keep their prices competitive. Andrew Carnegie and Henry Clay Frick, by the late 1880s the largest steel producers in the United States, were among the best at meeting such competitive challenge. During the first half of the decade, they reduced the cost of producing a ton of steel rails from $67.50 to $28.50.[17] Even competition could not keep them from making a handsome 13 percent profit on invested capital.[18]

All the same, by the mid-1880s, Frick and Carnegie had concluded that "the Amalgamated Association placed a tax on improvements, therefore, the Amalgamated had to go." Frick was convinced—and from a pure efficiency standpoint he may have been right—that the Carnegie mills had not reached maximum efficiency "because of Amalgamated men." He resolved to destroy the union and reorganize the mills "so that we shall not have to employ any more men than absolutely necessary."[19]

The sparring between Carnegie and Frick on one side, and the Amalgamated Association on the other, began in 1882, soon after Carnegie Steel's modern Homestead plant opened its doors. This mill had hardly been in operation for more than a few months when Carnegie began to pressure its men to leave the union. His employees, however, saw his pleas as harassment and walked off their jobs in protest. Carnegie backed down, at least for a while.[20]

Two years later, in the winter of 1884-1885, Carnegie tried a direct challenge with the workers of the older Edgar Thompson mill at Braddock, Pennsylvania. He closed his mill in order to modernize it, with an open hearth furnace chief among the new installations. The changes allowed Carnegie to dismiss 300 of

Edgar Thompson's 450 skilled workers. The resultant strike was quickly broken. Workers that Carnegie rehired were forced to accept substantial wage cuts. Steelworkers who had been paid $120 a month before the strike, so the men claimed, earned only $60 a month after it. With production resumed on his terms, Carnegie went after the Amalgamated's crippled local. In the winter of 1886-1887, he again closed the mill for "annual repairs" and did not reopen until all the men had signed iron clad contracts pledging to leave the union.[21]

After their Braddock victory, Carnegie and Frick temporarily halted their antiunion campaign in order to concentrate on modernizing their mills. In 1892, after having given the Amalgamated Association a five-year respite, they resumed the offensive. Homestead, Pennsylvania, became the scene for the final battle between the union and the steel magnates. Early that summer, Frick insisted that 325 skilled men accept a reduction in pay. The union was told that if it resisted, the Homestead plant would be run with nonunion labor. Having already accepted a substantial wage cut in 1889, the union refused to capitulate. On July 1, Frick replied by locking out the men. The workers in turn responded by seizing control of the mill and the city. When Frick imported 300 Pinkerton detectives to dislodge the strikers, the men stood ready to give armed resistance. A pitched battle, perhaps one of the bloodiest scenes of industrial warfare in American history, ensued. Before the Pinkertons were driven off, three of them were killed and thirty wounded. The strikers lost ten men before achieving what proved to be a pyrrhic victory. When the state governor sent the militia to Homestead to restore order, Frick broke the strike.[22]

The Homestead disaster, almost immediately followed by the depression of the 1890s, destroyed the Amalgamated Association. On November 17 when the men tried to return to work, two-thirds of the former strikers found that they had been replaced. When the Homestead plant resumed normal operations, Carnegie pledged that he would never again recognize the Amalgamated Association or any other labor organization.

He kept his word. Repeating the tactic perfected at Homestead, he began to close mills one at a time until all his employees agreed to sign iron clad nonunion contracts. Such agreements were enforced. Spies were hired to infiltrate union meetings. Men attending such meetings were immediately fired and blacklisted. Such spying made union organization virtually impossible because the men never knew whether they were speaking to one of their bosses' undercover agents. So intimidated were the workers that they would not even speak to reporters. Frightened men would flee in panic when they were approached for an interview, saying, as one reporter had it, "me no can talk, me work for company, me lose job." "Every man who is dependent on the steel companies for his living keeps his mouth shut, for fear a careless word may lose his job," one steelworker's wife declared.[23]

The union gone, management minimized labor costs by keeping wages low and hours long. By 1910, it had reduced labor costs to less than 17 percent of total costs.[24] No longer did steel magnates speak of the eight-hour day. Men like Carnegie and Frick were quite willing to drive their workers to the limits of human endurance twelve hours a day, seven days a week. The misery of such long hours was intensified by the club of the piecework system. Unskilled and semiskilled workers were divided into gangs supervised by "pushers" who were paid to make sure that the men worked as fast as possible. The pushers received bonuses if their gangs exceeded set goals. They and the foremen drove the men to compete for what bonus money remained. One bonus drive was followed by another as productivity demands were constantly raised. A reporter for *Munsey's Magazine* described the effects on the men: "In a few years the workmen are nervous wrecks, thrown on the street like squeezed lemons, after having set a standard of work that their unfortunate followers will have to maintain."[25]

The steelworkers bitterly recognized their plight. "Tell me how can a man get any pleasure out of working this way?" one asked two years after the Homestead strike. "I'm at work most of the day, and I'm so tired at night that I go to bed as soon as I've eaten supper. I've got ideas of what a home ought to be alright, but the way things are I just eat and sleep here." Another man found conditions equally inhumane, assuming that his interviewer accurately reported the substance of his thought, if not, exactly, his language: "The worst part of the whole business is this, it brutalizes a man," he declared. "You can't help it, you start in being a man, but more and more you become a machine and the pleasures are few and far between. It's like all severe labor, it drags you down morally and physically."[26]

The efficiency-minded mill owners cut tonnage rates as fast as worker productivity increased. On the average, the scales were reduced by 50 percent every five years. As production soared, it was inevitable, at least under capitalism, that tonnage rates would fall. If they had not been reduced, some men would have been earning several hundred dollars a week by 1910. In a free, nonunion labor market, management needed little dexterity to avoid such gains by their men. Avoiding gains, however, was not enough for the steel bosses. Between 1892 and 1897 tonnage rates were so drastically reduced that average annual wages actually fell by 20 percent, from $413 to $357.[27] This happened at a time when the steel mills, which were operating at unprecedented efficiency, were reducing the cost of steel rails by more than 50 percent.[28] Such increased productivity, together with reduced worker purchasing power, which had preoccupied Karl Marx among others, undoubtedly contributed to the economic crisis of the 1890s. By 1896 even Samuel Gompers of the AFL was angry. He declared that the depression had been caused by capitalists who demanded "production, production, production for prosperity at the expense of refusing to recognize the rights of the working class." He might very well have been directing his words at Carnegie, Frick, and the other steel barons.[29]

Samuel Gompers, of course, did not see radical politics as playing a role in the steelworkers' struggle. The election returns from Pennsylvania's sixteen largest steel communities show that most steelworkers agreed with him. In normal times, they appear to have concluded that there were no economic reasons to choose between the Democratic or Republican parties. So, they, like the rest of the electorate, divided along ethnic or religious lines. Steel towns, like Bethlehem, that were largely Catholic, tended to vote Democratic, while Protestant towns, like McKeesport, were Republican strongholds.[30]

During the 1870s and 1880s, the Democratic and Republican parties competed on an equal basis for the steelworker vote. The Republicans won pluralities in 1874 and 1876, the Democrats won in 1878, and the Republicans were again triumphant in 1880. The 1876 and 1878 elections were significant because their results show that the Greenback-Labor party was able to capitalize on the violent strikes of the period in order to capture 20 percent of the vote.[31] After the collapse of the Greenback party in 1880, elections continued to be closely fought, with the balance of power constantly moving back and forth between the Democratic and Republican parties. These political shifts were not caused by worker migration in and out of the steel towns. An examination of the manuscript census shows that the population was remarkably stable with steelworkers and their families tending to remain in the same town for several generations. They definitely were not part of Stephan Thernstrom's migratory proletariat.[32] The unstable political situation was not a function of an unstable population. It resulted from the fact that some steelworkers identified with neither the Democratic nor the Republican parties. In the closely fought elections of the 1880s, these voters held the balance of power—that is, until the realignment during the following decade when President Grover Cleveland's handling of the depression appears to have convinced most steelworkers, even many Catholics, to vote Republican. During the depressed 1890s, the Republican party often received as much as 65 percent of the steel town vote.[33] The Republican connection, however, was not a profitable one for the steel workers. Republican economic policy did not bring prosperity to them.

The situation in the coal industry during the 1880s and early 1890s was different from that of steel; from the workers' point of view, it was generally worse.[34] Before the depression of 1893, coal miners had not enjoyed the relative prosperity of their steel brethren. The depression in this industry thus hit men already living at or below the subsistence level. In 1888, the recently founded AFL unequivocally declared that "miners were worse off than any other workmen in the country."[35] Miners on starvation wages were also unemployed a good part of the time.

A man who dug coal in Clarion County, Pennsylvania, described how difficult it was to support a family on three days of work a week:

The conditions of the coal miners is a deplorable one in this locality. Their living consists of bread, coffee and boiling meat. There are miners' children here who never have shoes except for old ones they find in the streets and who are not able to attend school during the winter months for want of clothing to keep them warm. We do not see half enough work and for that about half pay.[36]

Conditions were no better in Westmoreland County where a miner complained:

The miners are not making a decent living by any means. Nor could they do so if they worked full time at the present price now paid. . . . We are not paying our way but going into debt every month. What few clothes we have are wearing out. Our names for honesty and uprightedness are getting tarnished and yet it is not our fault for we try to live within our incomes.[37]

Miners could not feed their family on the $300 to $350 a year they earned during the 1880s. "I am not a drunkard, spendthrift or a loafer," one Illinois miner declared. "Still I cannot make enough to live on."[38]

If coal miners, like steelworkers, had been permitted to patronize any store they wanted to, they might have been able to subsist even on as little as $350 a year. Quite probably from half to two-thirds of the coal miners, however, were forced to purchase at inflated prices food, clothing, pick axes, and blasting powder at a company store, and that on an income already cut one-fourth by high rent for ramshackle company-owned houses.[39] When mines had first opened in the wilderness, it had often been necessary for the operator to provide his employees with houses and stores to buy food and supplies. Thereafter, even though further settlement brought an independent community, operators usually insisted on keeping their stores open. Such establishments had almost always proved to be very profitable, since they charged anywhere from 10 to

40 percent higher than elsewhere.[40] Table 2.1, for example, shows the differences in 1896 between prices in town and company stores in Butchel, Ohio.[41]

Table 2.1
1896 PRICES IN TOWN AND COMPANY STORES, BUTCHEL, OHIO

Item	Town Store	Company Store
Flour	50-60¢/lb.	90¢/lb.
Coffee	18¢/lb.	24¢/lb.
Salt meat	61½¢/lb.	94¢/lb.
Oats	25¢/8 lbs.	25¢/4 lbs.
Potatoes	33½¢/bushel	60¢/bushel

Even in the well-developed towns like Butchel, the stores could charge such prices because the miners had little or no choice but to patronize them. They were expected to spend everything they earned at the company store. Those who refused to do so lost their jobs. "If you happen to strike a lucky streak some months and clear a few dollars, and come pay day you get a little cash, one miner complained, "the first thing that is rubbed in your face is that you are not buying enough from the company store, and if it happens again you will be discharged."[42] A committee of the Pennsylvania legislature investigated conditions in the state's coal towns and concluded that such miner complaints were justified. "Mine owners operate company stores in which excessive prices for goods are charged and compel the miners to deal therein," the committee reported.[43]

Accidents and death compounded the miseries of low wages, chronic unemployment, and company exploitation with housing and groceries. If a mining shaft collapsed, the men were usually hopelessly trapped. In lesser accidents, falling chunks of coal often crushed the men's arms and legs. Each year one of every 500 men who worked in the collieries perished underground, and one of every 125 was seriously injured. The injured received little or no compensation, just the penalties of more time off the job. The miners did have some success in persuading state legislatures to pass safety legislation, and inspectors were appointed to enforce such legislation, but the presence of the law did not appreciably reduce the coal industry's high accident rate.[44]

Life in America's coal towns made some immigrants from the British Isles sorry they had made the move to the "land of plenty." Many believed that a coal miner could live more comfortably in England than in the United States. One such disappointed immigrant wrote:

Six years since I came to this country with my wife and five children. I was able to pay their way over all along with me and I found enough money left when I got to my destination for purchasing all the necessities for starting housekeeping. . . . Were I to sell everything I possessed, I could not pay the debts I owe, much less get back to England. In England I worked but six hours at the rate of $1.40 per day, with a house, garden and coal. Here a miner gets to work a few months a year and consequently has to work all the hours that God sends him, in fact make a beast of burden of himself or starve. . . . In England, operators build reading rooms and lecture halls to which everybody has free access. Here we don't need them for while we are working we can't think of anything else but work.

Another Englishman had similar regrets:

I worked for Coalney's coal company. These works are 16 miles from Glasgow. I worked for them from 1851 to 1868. I emphatically say that I was better off there than I have been ever since I worked in this country. Eight hours constituted a day's work. Here I see men working 14, 16, 18 hours a day trying to make a living.[45]

Even if the operators who owned bituminous coal mines in the Central Competitive Field—Illinois, Indiana, Ohio, and western Pennsylvania—had wanted to pay their employees a decent wage, it would have been very difficult for them to have done so. Their industry was plagued by overproduction in terms of the existing market. Because not much capital was required to open a colliery, thousands of aspiring entrepreneurs entered the coal industry. As one Pittsburgh coal operator put it, "Anybody can go into the coal business . . . because you only have to dig a hole in the ground . . . and bring up the coal."[46] By the mid-1880s, there was a glut; the industry's capacity exceeded existing demand by about 50 percent. Nor could the thousands of operators significantly cut production in order to bring stability to the industry. Each operator, too small to influence the market, could only reduce prices in a desperate effort to sell coal. In steel, many, perhaps most, owners were able to keep profits high by cutting wages and introducing technological innovations. But coal mine owners operated a labor-intensive industry that was slow to modernize. Consequently, few of them earned more than 3 or 4 percent profit on their invested capital.[47] Their perspective was far different from that of the steel magnates.

For coal, cut-throat competition was a disaster that depressed both profits and wages. This was particularly true in the Central Competitive Field, which together with West Virginia produced more than 70 percent of the coal mined in the United States.[48] Coal mine owners desperately sought to limit competition and equalize their costs. Market conditions, of course, contributed to the competitive framework of the bituminous coal industry, as did transportation costs, which were determined by the distances of the mines from their markets. Operators with collieries relatively close to Chicago, Detroit, Cleveland, and Toledo had a distinct advantage. Sometimes, however, geology was more important than geography. It was less expensive to extract coal from the thick-seamed mines in southern Illinois, Ohio, and western Pennsylvania than it was from the thin-seamed mines found elsewhere. Also mining machinery could be used profitably only in thick-seamed mines. It was estimated that such machinery increased profits by between 8 and 18 percent.[49]

This was minor, however, when compared to the savings that could be realized by cutting labor costs. Competition, therefore, always resulted in battles to reduce wages. When one operator cut wages, his competitors had no choice but to follow. This cycle usually ended with all the operators in the same competitive position as they had been before. The only difference was that wages and coal prices had been reduced.

By 1885, the bituminous coalfields were in such a chaotic

state that the desperate coal operators were willing to work with organized labor to bring stability to the industry. These men, on the verge of bankruptcy, hoped that a union contract that would bind them all to a fixed wage scale would make it impossible for any one of them to cut prices and undersell competitors. On October 15, 1885, a few colliery owners in Illinois, Indiana, and Ohio met with the executive board of the National Federation of Miners and Mine Laborers. They decided to invite all the nation's soft-coal mine operators to attend a joint conference of miners and operators. The invitation recognized the ill consequences for both owners and miners of the overproduction, intense competition, and wage and price cuts and went on to the quite remarkable conclusion:

If the price of labor in the United States was uniformly raised to the standard of three years ago, the employers of labor would occupy toward each other in point of competition, the same relative position as at the present. Such a general advance would be beneficial to their interests and would materially remove the general discontent of the miners in their employment.[50]

Most of the owners in the Central Competitive Field responded favorably. On February 23, 1886, miners and operators from Ohio, Indiana, Illinois, and Pennsylvania met at Columbus, Ohio, and agreed upon a scale of wages for the entire midwestern bituminous coal region. The convention was guided by a principle of competitive equality: the wages each operator paid his employees was, within fixed limits, to be based on his production and marketing costs.[51]

The hopes of the miners and operators that the Joint Conference would bring order and stability were soon disappointed. From the start, the agreement proved to be unstable because enough operators had stayed away from the Columbus convention to threaten the system.[52] Some of the opponents were philosophically opposed to dealing with organized labor, while others, not necessarily opposed to collective bargaining, were unwilling to subordinate their interests to those of the industry. The coal mine owners of southern Illinois presented a special problem. They had many natural advantages they were loathe to forfeit. Not only did they have special agreements with the railroads to ship their coal cheaply, but their collieries had thick veins that could be easily worked by mining machinery. Fearing that the Joint Conference would cut into these natural advantages, the southern Illinois operators preferred to deal with their miners as they had in the past and refused to adhere to competitive equality.[53]

The not entirely unexpected attitude of the southern Illinois operators made their nearest competitors in northern Illinois uneasy. Reluctantly attending the Columbus convention, they had given only conditional approval to its work and insisted that the agreement would not go into effect unless southern Illinois was brought in. Yet only a strike by the union had a chance of doing this. The Federation of Miners and Mine Laborers, however, represented only 20 percent of the coal miners and did not feel strong enough to risk a suspension. Southern Illinois therefore remained outside the Joint Conference, putting the agreement for the entire Central Competitive Field in jeopardy.[54]

Labor was hesitant about trying to enforce the agreement because it, like management, was also badly divided. At Columbus, the bulk of the miners were represented by the Federation of Miners and Mine Laborers, an affiliate of the AFL, which had been founded that year. In southern Illinois and Pennsylvania, however, most of the unionized miners owed allegiance to the older Knights of Labor. Incipient intraunion rivalry was blunted when the two unions agreed upon a united front when dealing with the operators. In any particular area the organization with the largest membership was to be responsible for strikes and grievances. The Federation and the Knights pledged themselves to "use every honest and fair means to induce every miner to become a member of one or the other."[55]

The agreement was much easier to make than to keep. The leadership of the Knights, seeing the Joint Conference as the child of the rival Federation, often did its best to undercut the agreement. It signed contracts for wages lower than union scale. The Knights claimed that it was impossible to enforce the union scale so long as 60 percent of the coal was being dug by nonunion labor.[56]

It was the Illinois situation, however, that eventually destroyed not only the truce between the Knights and the Federation but the Joint Conference as well. In 1889, the northern Illinois operators refused to participate in the conference, and the entire system quickly broke down. The crisis thus caused once again made the leadership of the Knights and the Federation realize that they had to work together. Another peace meeting was held in January 1890 that led to the founding of the United Mine Workers (UMW). As an AFL affiliate, the new union immediately began trying to revive the Joint Conference. The operators, disillusioned by past experience, were not interested. Although the UMW's first impulse was to call a strike, a meeting of district officials decided that a union that still represented only 20 percent of the nation's soft-coal miners could not do so. Several more years of organizational efforts plus the wage cuts of a severe depression would be needed to bring them to that mark.

Adding to the pressures for union militancy were the cutting machines that the operators had begun to introduce during the late 1880s. Such machinery, which by 1899 was operating in 35 percent of the midwestern coal mines, displaced many skilled pick miners.[57] In addition, for the bituminous coal industry as a whole, the cutting machines brought a further glut to the market. Before their arrival, two pick miners, working together, usually had dug about six tons of coal a day, but a cutting machine by 1892 was able to cut fifty tons a day, with but seven men to tend it.[58] Many operators could thus reduce their labor force by as much as one-third. The machines made an already severe unemployment problem critical.[59]

The technological transformation in coal came more slowly than it had in steel, yet the change was probably as traumatic for coal miners as for Carnegie's puddlers. The pick miner of the 1880s was usually poor, but before mechanization, his work, like that of the skilled steelworkers, had its nonmonetary compensations. Most of the miners had been fiercely independent skilled craftsmen. They had learned their trade as boys by loading coal their fathers cut. Family traditions and techniques were proudly preserved and handed down from one generation to another. People who visited the collieries were struck by the "geometric exactness" with which the coal was cut. Miners found satisfaction comparing their methods with those of a neighbor. Men who as boys in Durham, England, had learned to cut coal vertically went out of their way to impress Welshmen, who cut coal horizontally, with the superiority of their technique. It may be that the joys of this competition were increased by the heated arguments and fistfights occasionally reported.[60]

These proud men further resembled the early skilled steelworkers in not only demanding but receiving respect from their bosses and foremen. Assigned to a vein, they often worked without supervision. Foremen, supposed to boss over a hundred men scattered throughout a colliery, could not possibly watch all. Generally nobody tried to make sure that men reported for work by a certain time. Foremen often did not know when their men took days off. Assuming that the pick miners who worked under them were competent, foremen permitted them to work at their own pace. A supervisor might offer advice to a miner, but such suggestions were rarely given, much less received, as reprimands. When a supervisor visited a miner, the man might well assert his independence by stopping work and sitting down. The miners, much like skilled steelworkers, were largely their bosses in the pits.[61]

Mechanization quickly ended this independence. The cutting machines manned by seven or eight men would go from room to room cutting coal. When the machine left, loaders, many of them displaced pick miners, would load the coal into cars. Soon thousands of once-proud craftsmen were trailing after the machines. An industrial commission appointed by President William McKinley caught the pathos of the situation. "The mining machine is in fact," said the commission, "the natural enemy of the coal miners; it destroys the value of their skill and experience, obliterates their trade and reduces them to the ranks of common laborers." Facts and figures supported the commission's findings. In hand mines, 70 percent of the labor force were skilled pick miners, earning between $2.72 and $3.21

a day; the unskilled laborers, who loaded coal and helped the
pick miners with other tasks, earned $1.75 a day. In machine
mines, however, 70 percent of the labor force were loaders,
earning $1.75 a day; 9.31 percent were cutting machine operators,
earning $2.28 a day; while only 20.69 percent were pick miners,
earning $2.53 a day.[62]

Former pick miners, unimpressed by the increased efficiency they were by and large paying for, complained bitterly
about their plight. A man from DuBois, Pennsylvania, moaned
that while he and his fellow pick miners were idle, "the machines
[were] . . . working every day." W. A. Crawford, president of
the UMW's Illinois district, warned that the union had "reached
a crisis." "We must do something with the machine miners
or else be dragged down into the seething abyss of hunger and
poverty."[63]

When the mining machines were first introduced to Ohio
in 1884, the pick miners had tried to do something about them.
The scene was the Hocking Valley where 70 percent of the
state's coal was dug. As fast as the operators introduced the
new mining machines, they reduced wages. In the spring of
1884, pick miner tonnage rates were cut from 70 cents to 60
cents, and then to 50 cents. Weekly take-home pay was reduced
even more rapidly, from $27.53 in March to $18.55 in April, to
$17.95 in May, and finally to $12.83 in June. On June 23, the
miners struck. Occupying the mines, they immediately destroyed
many of the new cutting machines.[64] The strike lasted for nine
months. Armed strikers, resolved to win even against heavy
odds, attacked strikebreakers as well as the trains that were
bringing them into the valley. Hunger in time made the men
and their families only more determined. Even the severe
winter of 1884-1885, during which many strikers subsisted on
"mush and goats milk," did not break their spirits. The men
held out until February 1885, when the strike was settled by
arbitration. The state arbitrators forced the operators to increase
wages by 10 cents a ton and made them promise to consider
the pick miner when introducing mining machinery. The hard-
won promise may have looked good, yet the operators continued
to replace the pick miners with cutting machines as fast as
they became available.

The Hocking Valley was not the only place where cutting machines led to embittered labor relations. In the late 1880s and early 1890s, strikes became part of the soft-coal miners' way of life. Even during the relatively prosperous years between 1887 and 1893, there were 350 strikes in the Central Competitive Field. Each year tens of thousands of men walked the picket lines. The coal miners seemed constantly to be either striking or thinking about striking. Demanding an increase in wages, they would walk off their jobs in the winter when the price of coal was rising. In the spring, they might strike again to resist a reduction. Many years later, an Ohio miner described labor-management relations during this period. "We would strike [for] three, four or six months; go back to work when starved to it; work until we had a barrel of flour and a side of bacon and then give them another tussle."[65]

The UMW, though it tried, often lost control over the militant miners, not surprisingly since only 20,000 of 125,000 carried union cards.[66] Table 2.2, which shows that less than 50 percent of the work stoppages staged between 1887 and 1893 were sanctioned by the UMW, documents the turbulence of a period in which more than 2 million man-days were lost as a result of strikes.[67]

Table 2.2
STRIKES IN THE BITUMINOUS COALFIELD, 1887-1893

Number of strikes	350
Number of places closed	2,692
Man-days lost (estimated)	2,055,000
Average duration of strike	45 days
Percent called by union	47 percent

In the 1890s, steelworkers went to the picket lines and ended up losing their union. The striking coal miners, on the other hand, did not face the concentrated and ruthless power of Andrew Carnegie and Henry Clay Frick. So despite the deprivation they faced while out of work, they struck again and again.

And hungry they were. A reporter for the *Chicago Herald,* who visited the homes of some strikers in Knightsville, Indiana, asserted "it [was] . . . an absolute fact . . . that the strikers and their families have been for the last two weeks trying to keep body and soul together on one meal a day." The Knightsville strikers were more fortunate than most, for they had built homes that they could mortgage for food. One of them spoke about the price of such survival:

There are three hundred of us in Knightsville and nearly all of these little huts you see around here were put up by us, but we are losing our hold on them and I'll tell you how. Nearly all of these little places are mortgaged to the store who kept the wolf away from our door during the last strike and who is giving us credit now too. If it was not for the little ones we would have heavy hearts, but after all the sight of the young ones encourages us to keep up this struggle.

The miners of Spring Valley, locked out on April 29, 1889, were more typical than the men and women of Knightsville. They had no homes to mortgage for food. Still they were determined to win. Surviving for months without pay, they refused to work even when offered terms. The strikers, many critically ill after an eight-month dispute, paid the price for their resolve. By August, "death [hung] . . . over the town. From a cursory examination it [was] . . . a low estimate that seven of every ten families [were] . . . sick, seriously so," a reporter for the *New York World* observed. One miner explained why the men refused to capitulate:

I fought for the negroes [in the Civil War] and now I am fighting for the folks. It is the principle of the thing I am starving for. I am an American citizen and I claim the right to educate my children as Americans should be educated. We offered to go to work for a year without a cent if the company would only keep us in food, send our children to school and pay the rent. . . . They wouldn't do it and that shows we cannot live on the reduced wages without begging or going into debt.[69]

The men, women, and children of Spring Valley could not hold out forever. The bitter cold of mid-December forced them back to work on the company's terms—a 20 percent reduction in pay. Yet the 1889 settlement was only a truce brought about by starvation. Eighteen months later the Spring Valley miners were again walking the picket lines.

All of the 350 strikes of the era did not result in as much suffering as did the Spring Valley affair, but violence and its legacy of bitterness accompanied many of them. The operators went to great lengths to keep their collieries open. Armed men were hired to escort strikebreakers through the picket lines. When they could, the miners armed themselves and fought back. The situation amounted to industrial warfare.

The war remained a matter of skirmishes until 1894, when the full force of the depression hit the industry. The crisis forced the UMW leadership to call upon all the miners to strike. So in 1894, and again in 1897, even though during the first case the UMW had only 23,000 members and $2,600 in its treasury, the miners of the Central Competitive Field struck. With over 100,000 men walking the picket lines, all but a few collieries were forced to close.

A strike, however, could neither end the depression nor force the operators, many on the verge of bankruptcy, to increase wages. As the depression worsened and factories closed their doors, the demand for coal fell, reducing its price by almost 20 percent. Collieries cut back on production, laying off thousands of miners. Those men who were lucky enough to continue working had to absorb one wage cut after another. Coal miners, who in 1893 had earned on the average $383 a year, found themselves by 1896 earning only $282. This represented a 20 percent reduction in real wages.[70]

Coal miners were bewildered by the speed at which tonnage rates fell. Men who had been paid between 70 and 75 cents a ton for coal in 1893 were earning only 45 cents a ton in 1897. At such a rate, even the working miners faced starvation. A reporter for the *Indiana Union* described the way families of such miners lived:

These people were pinched and eaten by the need for food, one might tell it in their eyes, large wild and wolfishly bright. . . . There were households of five and six with aggregate earnings which did not reach $100 during the twelve months last past. They were hopelessly ragged and beyond all hungry, thin and grimy, six, eight as high as ten living in a room unfit for swine.[71]

This was the way coal miners lived during the crisis of the 1890s. The downward spiral was not arrested until 1898, when, after a two-month strike, the operators were persuaded to revive the Joint Conference and increase wages.

During the 1890s, turbulent for steel and the bituminous coalfields, there was peace in the anthracite region of eastern Pennsylvania. Since most hard coal was used to heat homes rather than for industrial purposes, depression demand for anthracite coal remained relatively stable. In fact, between 1890 and 1897, its price actually rose from $3.71 to $4.01 a ton.[72] If the anthracite industry, like the bituminous industry, had been competitive, the price of hard coal would have never remained at such a high level. But with virtually all the nation's hard coal concentrated in less than 500 square miles of eastern Pennsylvania, the industry was a prime candidate for monopoly. The eastern railroads, whose post-Civil War expansion had opened up vast new markets for anthracite coal, took advantage of the situation. By the 1890s, six railroads, all controlled by the Morgan and Vanderbilt interests, owned 99 percent of the collieries in eastern Pennsylvania. Anthracite, therefore, did not fall prey to cutthroat competition and market overproduction. On the contrary, the price of coal was meticulously set by determining the volume of production and allotting tonnage quotas.[73]

In anthracite, wages were not at the mercy of the business cycle. Even during the depressed 1890s, they remained relatively stable. In 1890, the average anthracite coal miner earned $318.50 a year; seven years later he was still earning $317.22. During this period his standard of living actually rose as the prices he and his family paid fell by 5 percent. Table 2.3 shows the remarkable stability of conditions during years of boom or bust.[74]

Table 2.3
WAGES OF ANTHRACITE COAL MINERS, 1890-1896

Year	Hourly Wage	Days Worked	Average Annual Wage
1890	18.3ᵉ	204	$318.20
1891	19.0	200	330.60
1892	19.4	203	337.54
1893	19.4	198	329.28
1894	19.6	197	329.00
1895	19.6	190	317.52
1896	19.6	196	317.22

An industry that had so stabilized wages could conduct labor-management relations peaceably. In sharp contrast to Pennsylvania's bituminous coalfields, where 188,178 men were involved in 104 strikes between 1890 and 1894, the anthracite mines were struck only 45 times, with 21,532 men walking off their jobs.[75]

Peace, however, was very tenuous. Wages had been stabilized, but at a very low level. This precarious stability was shattered at the end of the depression, when immigrants from southern and eastern Europe, whose numbers had been steadily increasing since the mid-1880s, finally glutted the labor market. Between 1891 and 1897, when the amount of anthracite coal being dug increased by only 4 percent, the industry's available labor force grew by 23 percent from 126,000 to 150,000 men. Rather than increasing production in order to employ the growing labor force, the Morgan and Vanderbilt interests maintained output at depression levels to ensure high prices. The result was chronic underemployment. Miners, who during the early 1890s were employed 200 days a year, were working only 150 days by 1898. Average yearly wages consequently fell from $318 in 1890 to $270 nine years later.[76]

Thus, just when steel, the bituminous coalfields, and the rest of the nation were emerging from the depression, wages in anthracite began to fall. The protests of the hard-coal miner began to sound similar to those of his bituminous counterpart. "How can I raise a family," one man asked, "on two days a week sometimes and sometimes three days a week, keep house and pay for fuel and coal?"[77] Another veteran miner exclaimed: "We were just able to live on our wages before, but now most of us just have to eat less. I could not live if my sons and two daughters were not working. No married man can live on a coal miner's wages these days unless his children work too."[78]

The surplus of labor in eastern Pennsylvania not only reduced the anthracite coal miners' standard of living but enabled the operators to increase the demands they made on their employees. In a letter to the *Scranton Times,* one miner described working conditions under the new regime:

It has been stated that there has been no reduction in the mines during the last five years. Is this true? Most emphatically not. It is true that there has not been a general reduction, but a reduction has taken place all the same. The difference is that it has been given to the miner on the installment plan, i.e. one shaft, one vein would be reduced this month, and another the next month. [Payment for] rock work and timbering have been reduced to less than one-half during the last five years. A few years ago, the miner was paid for extra work, such as bailing out water, clearing falls in the road, clearing gobs, and many other things, but now he is told to do this for little or nothing. The chief element of this system has been brought about by the system of district bosses, who have become competitive in their devilish work of robbing the working man.

It is safe to say that the standard of wages of every position in the coal mine has been reduced in its wage earning value. A mine that required two or three driver bosses is now run with one driver boss and one or more assistants. A vacancy occurs in the position of runner and a good smart mule driver is promoted to the position, but not to the salary.[79]

Since the immigrants, who usually were forced to work for less money than English-speaking miners, appeared to be responsible for the deterioration of working conditions and the depressed wage scales, ethnic antagonisms became acute.

The influx of immigrants was as traumatic for anthracite miners as the introduction of mining machines had been for bituminous miners. Fortunately neither anthracite nor bituminous miners had to cope with both mining machines and immigrants. Anthracite coal was too hard to be cut by machine, while most of those immigrants interested in coal mining did not have the resources to migrate to the more distant bituminous fields. In 1900, when 60 percent of the anthracite industry's labor force had become of south or east European origin, only 20 percent of the nation's bituminous coal miners were new immigrants.[80]

English-speaking anthracite miners often hated the new immigrants as much as the bituminous miners hated the mining machines. One man took time out to tell John Mitchell, UMW president, how he felt:

I want to bid you God's speed in your grand work to restrict immigration to our beloved land of all those scum from the cities of Europe. . . . Our good hard working people have been driven from our old places of residence for we cannot live among them as they have taken the bread out of our mouths and our children have suffered hunger.

Another miner begged Mitchell "to do all in your power to restrict these bums and vandals, and don't let them into [the mines] with their shovels. . . . It is life or death for us. It is those foreigners that have ruined our country, not the late panic."[81]

The coming of the new immigrants certainly forced changes on many pick miners accustomed to respect as skilled craftsmen. The largely unskilled immigrants required foremen to be more vigilant in their supervision, and the English-speaking miners fell increasingly under the same discipline. Men who had once set their own hours now had to work regular hours. Peter Gallagher, a veteran of fifteen years in the mines, bitterly resented being told that "if you are not there before seven o'clock in the morning there will be no work for you." Gallagher recalled the many times in recent years when he was "staggering on the gangway from working in bad air" and the boss would threaten to discharge him if he "did not work until seven or

eight o'clock at night."[82] Such long hours were usually unnecessary because there was not enough work to keep them
busy for twelve hours. Nevertheless the miners were required
to report to work at dawn, even if there were no cars to be
loaded with coal at that hour. They would then have to stand
around, inhaling coal dust. Paid by the ton, they received no
compensation for this time. D. H. Dettery declared that after
"entering the mines at seven in the morning," he would often
"lay there until two o'clock without receiving a mine car," but
"if he tried to go home," he would be "suspended that day and
twenty more in addition."[83]

For the immigrants, who by the turn of the century accounted
for more than half of the industry's work force, conditions were
probably even harsher than they were for native-born workers.
While most English-speaking miners were skilled and generally
worked on a contract basis, the immigrants usually were common
laborers who loaded coal into mine cars and did the other work
that was necessary to prepare shafts for pick miners. Their pay
usually averaged one-third of the coal miner. This relationship
between the pick miners and the unskilled immigrant laborers
bred class and ethnic antagonism, which made worker solidarity
difficult to achieve.[84]

It was these immigrant miners who in 1897 shattered the
uneasy peace that prevailed in the anthracite region. The trouble
began when Gomer Jones, a superintendent at a colliery owned
by the Lehigh-Wilkes-Barre Railroad, expressed his determination to increase the severity of mine discipline. He boldly asserted:

When I came here a year ago, I came to restore discipline in the mines
and to operate them [profitably]. The discipline was lax and the men did
as they pleased. The two superintendents here then associated with the
men, mixed with them, and were regarded as hail fellows, well met. . . .
Well now, I cannot do that. I am not a drinking man, and I have never
made it a practice to hobnob with the men. . . . When I give an order
I expect them to be obeyed. . . . I dismissed a good many men, about
80 I think, but never put any in their place.[85]

On August 13, the miners responded to Jones's arrogance by
striking. This rebellion was initiated by the Slavic and Italian

miners who were the most affected by Jones's dictatorial discipline. Demanding an end to this new regime and an increase in wages, they organized militant picket lines, an action that stunned the coal mine owners, who raised wages at once, hoping to defuse an explosive situation.[86]

The concession did not buy peace. The successful militancy of the men proved to be contagious. Five hundred Slavs employed at the nearby Van Winckle colliery struck, saying that they would no longer work for less money than English-speaking miners. By early September, the entire Wilkes—Barre-Scranton area was paralyzed as 11,000 men picketed. When the coal companies refused to negotiate with the strikers, the men and their families began to march from one colliery to another, threatening to destroy any mine that continued to dig coal. When the strikers encountered policemen determined to stop their marches, they shouted, "Getta outa de way. We noa stoppa."[87]

At that point, the police and the coal mine owners resolved to restore law and order. Lattimer was the scene of the inevitable clash. It occurred when a group of miners from Harwood, marching to Lattimer to close down a colliery, were met by the sheriff and his armed deputies. It is not entirely clear whether the sheriff fell or was pushed, but when he hit the ground, he ordered his deputies to open fire on the strikers. When the smoke cleared, nineteen miners were dead and thirty wounded.[88] The Lattimer massacre intimidated the miners and helped break the strike. Afraid to organize any more mass demonstrations, the strikers were forced to return to work on their bosses' terms.

The 1897 anthracite strike was spontaneous; UMW had almost nothing to do with organizing it. The union had great difficulty organizing miners divided by ethnic antagonisms. Even though the English-speaking miners had seen conditions deteriorate, they wanted nothing to do with a union that treated "Americans" and Slavs as equals. Union men met with only mixed success when they pleaded for unity with the "foreigners" who were "miners and fellow sufferers."[89]

Slavic and Italian immigrants, on the other hand, greeted

the union warmly. When the UMW began to employ Slavic and Italian organizers and distribute foreign-language literature, it discovered that the new immigrants would walk miles to attend a meeting or a rally. One union man, working out of the tiny community of Marshwood, described the response he received:

This is an isolated place, several miles from any other town in the woods on the Moosic mountain, but several foreign speaking people have been walking from Jessup and Olymphant, some five miles away, to attend local union meetings, and at the same time talking unionism to their friends in the mines and through their noble efforts we organized a branch in this little town with 76 members.[90]

The militancy of the Slavic and Italian immigrants guaranteed the union's success, despite the hostility of the English-speaking miners. By 1900, when almost 70 percent of the men who dug coal in eastern Pennsylvania were new immigrants, the anthracite region was effectively unionized. In 1902, after six years of bitter labor-management strife, the UMW forced the operators to grant it de facto recognition.

Thus while the Amalgamated Association of Iron and Steel Workers was being smashed in a rapidly modernizing steel industry, the UMW marched from one victory to another. The chaotic market condition of the Central Competitive Field eventually contributed to the union's success. Buoyed by its victory in soft coal, the UMW had turned its attention to the anthracite region. Here, where a handful of railroads monopolized the coal industry, unionization met with stiff resistance before triumphing. The other part of the story is how this struggle for union recognition helped lead both the soft- and hard-coal miners to radical political activity.

NOTES

1. U.S. Department of Commerce, Bureau of the Census, *Abstract of the Census of Manufactures, 1914* (Washington, D.C.: Government Printing Office, 1917), pp. 17-29.

2. Quoted in Harold U. Faulkner, *Politics, Reform and Expansion* (New York: Harper and Row, 1959), p. 141.

3. Charles Hoffmann, "The Depression of the Nineties," *Journal of Economic History* 16 (June 1956):138-41; Samuel Rezneck, "The Depression of the Nineties—An Economic History" (Ph.D. diss., Columbia University, 1954), pp. 102-16; Philip Foner, *The Politics and Policies of the American Federation of Labor* (New York: International, 1961), p. 13.

4. The 1900 census ranked the coal industry behind the iron and steel, textile, lumber, food, and paper industries. Bureau of the Census, *Abstract of the Census of Manufactures,* pp. 17-18, 24; Peter Temin, *Iron and Steel in Nineteenth Century America* (Cambridge: Harvard University Press, 1964), p. 270; U.S. Immigration Commission, *Immigrants in Industries* (Washington, D.C.: Government Printing Office, 1911), 6:3, 16:587 (hereafter cited as U.S. Immigration Commission).

5. Temin, *Iron and Steel,* pp. 125-32.

6. Robert Bruce, *1877: Year of Violence* (Indianapolis: Bobbs-Merrill, 1959).

7. Jesse Robinson, *The Amalgamated Association of Iron and Steel Workers* (Baltimore: Johns Hopkins University Press, 1920).

8. *See* article by Jack Em in the *National Labor Tribune* 1, July 3, 1899; Leon Wolff, *Lockout: The Story of the Homestead Strike of 1892* (New York: Harper and Row, 1965), p. 42.

9. Wolff, *Lockout,* pp. 40-47; U.S. Bureau of Labor Statistics, *Bulletin 604: History of Real Wages in the United States, from Colonial Times to 1928* (Washington, D.C.: Government Printing Office, 1932); *see* appendix A.

10. Pennsylvania Secretary for Internal Affairs, *Annual Report, 1882-83* (Harrisburg: State Printers, 1884), 16:131.

11. Wolff, *Lockout,* pp. 40-43. *See* David Montgomery, *Workers Control in America* (Cambridge: Cambridge University Press, 1979), pp. 1-31.

12. Robinson, *Amalgamated Association,* pp. 97-100; Wolff, *Lockout,* p. 41; *National Labor Tribune,* April 7, 1876, March 12, 1878, March 22, 1879; "Proceedings of the 1878 Annual Convention of the Amalgamated Association of Iron and Steel Workers," pp. 176-77; on temperance see *National Labor Tribune,* February 3, 9, 1877, February 7, 1878.

13. Quoted in Pennsylvania Secretary for Internal Affairs, *Annual Report, 1882-83,* 3:132.

14. Robinson, *Amalgamated Association,* p. 132.

15. David Brody, *Steel Workers in America: The Non-Union Era* (Cambridge: Harvard University Press, 1969), pp. 10-12.

16. Ibid., p. 13; Peter Doeinger, "Piece Rate Wage Structure in the Pittsburgh Iron and Steel Industry," *Labor History* 9 (Spring 1968): 42-78; U.S. Commissioner of Labor, *Sixth Annual Report* (Washington, D.C.: Government Printing Office, 1891), pp. 336-54.

17. Temin, *Iron and Steel,* p. 283.

18. Melvin Urofsky, *Big Steel and the Wilson Administration* (Columbus: Ohio State University Press, 1969), p. xxxi; Horace Wilgus, *The United States Steel Corporation* (Chicago: Calaghan, 1901), p. 212.

19. Henry Clay Frick quoted in David Brody, *Labor in Crisis: The Steel Strike of 1919* (Philadelphia: Lippincott, 1965), p. 17.

20. John Fitch, *The Steel Workers* (New York: Charities Publication Committee, 1910), p. 110.

21. Ibid., p. 115; Robinson, *Amalgamated Association,* p. 125; interview with Mr. Phillips in David Saposs, "Interviews with Steel Workers" (done during the summer of 1920 and deposited at the Wisconsin State Historical Society); *National Labor Tribune,* February 7, 1885, May 5, 1888; David Novak and Richard Perlman, "Wages in Iron and Steel," *Journal of Economic History* 23 (September 1962):45-62.

22. The best account of the strike is Wolff, *Lockout; see also* Arthur Burgoyne, *Homestead* (Pittsburgh: Rawsthrone, 1893); for an eyewitness account see *New York Tribune* 1, July 1-30, 1892.

23. Interview with J. R. Root, in Saposs, "Interviews with Steel Workers."

24. Twenty years earlier the labor component had been about 30 percent greater at 22.5 percent. Brody, *Labor in Crisis,* p. 15; Fitch, *Steel Workers,* pp. 139-50.

25. Herbert Casson, "Romance of Iron and Steel in America," *Munsey's Magazine* 22 (October 1906):26.

26. Hamlin Garland, "Homestead and Its Perilous Trades," *McClure's Magazine* 22 (June 1894):9-12.

27. Figures compiled from Paul Douglas, *Real Wages in the United States, 1890-1926* (Boston: Houghton Mifflin, 1930); Albert Rees, *Real Wages in Manufacturing* (Princeton: Princeton University Press, 1961), p. 61; *see* appendices B and C; for tonnage rates *see* U.S. Immigration Commission, 8:448-52. During these depression years, prices paid by steelworkers fell by 5 percent; *see* appendix C.

28. Temin, *Iron and Steel,* p. 284.

29. Quoted in Faulkner, *Politics of Reform,* p. 184.

30. Appendix 0; National Archives, "Manuscript Census," 1880 and 1900 (microfilm edition) [hereafter cited as "Manuscript Census."

31. "Manuscript Census."

32. Coal miners also do not fit into Thernstrom's model. The manuscript census clearly shows that they tended to form stable communities. Their families usually remained in one town from one generation to the next. Most of the newcomers to Pennsylvania and Ohio's coal towns were European immigrants. There was virtually no internal migration of American-born coal miners. "Manuscript Census," 1880 and 1900.

33. Appendix O.

34. There were really two coal industries: bituminous and anthracite. Bituminous or soft coal, which accounted for about 75 percent of the coal dug in the United States, is now found in every region of the country, but in the 1880s and 1890s more than 90 percent of the nation's soft coal was mined in the so-called Central Competitive Field: western Pennsylvania, Illinois, Indiana, and Ohio. Much of the bituminous coal mined in western Pennsylvania melts readily and burns with particularly intense heat. This coal can be baked into coke, a brittle fuel with a high percentage of carbon, which is used in the manufacture of steel. Consequently, by the early 1880s, the steel companies began acquiring western Pennsylvania's coking coal mines. While useful for industrial purposes, bituminous coal burns with too much smoke to be suitable for domestic heating. For this, anthracite coal, found in eastern Pennsylvania, is preferred.

35. Quoted in Henry D. Lloyd, *A Strike of Millionaires against Miners* (Springfield: Bedford Clarke, 1890), p. 9.

36. Pennsylvania Secretary for Internal Affairs, *Annual Report, 1882-83,* 3:123.

37. Ibid., p. 132.

38. Arthur Suffern, *Conciliation and Arbitration in the Coal Industry* (Boston: Houghton Mifflin, 1915), pp. 354-65.

39. Miner quoted in *Chicago Herald,* as quoted in the *United Mine Workers Journal,* December 24, 1891 (hereafter cited as *UMWJ*).

40. It is difficult, if not impossible, to determine how many coal miners lived in company houses and were forced to patronize company stores. Most miners who lived in larger towns and cities like Carbondale, Illinois, in the bituminous region, or Wilkes-Barre and Scranton, in the anthracite region, were permitted to live and buy where they pleased. However, most smaller mining communities were company towns. I estimate that about two-thirds of the bituminous and one-half of the anthracite miners lived in such communities. Peter Roberts, *Anthracite Coal Communities* (New York: Traeger, 1904), pp. 33-46.

41. *UMWJ*, January 30, 1896, p. 2.

42. Ibid., December 21, 1897, p. 2.

43. Report quoted in ibid., June 10, 1897, p. 2.

44. *See* appendix D. Most states began to pass mine safety legislation during the 1870s and 1880s. On the surface, these figures might have appeared acceptable. However, upon closer examination, one sees that a coal miner who spent twenty-five years working underground had a one in twenty chance of dying on the job and a one in five chance of being seriously injured.

45. Pennsylvania Secretary for Internal Affairs, *Annual Report, 1885* (Harrisburg: State Printers, 1886), 3:127-29.

46. U.S. Industrial Commission, *Final Report* (Washington, D.C., Government Printing Office, 1900-1902), pp. 12, 87. Conditions in the anthracite industry were quite different from those that are now being described.

47. U.S. Department of the Interior, Census Office, *Report on Mineral Industries in the United States at the 11th Census* (Washington, D.C.: Government Printing Office, 1892), p. 347. In 1890, wages represented 22.5 percent of the cost of manufacturing steel; however, labor accounted for 74.1 percent of the cost of digging coal. U.S. Department of the Interior, Census Office, *Report on Mineral Resources in the United States at the 11th Census, 1890* (Washington, D.C.: Government Printing Office, 1891), p. 3477.

48. *Eighteenth Annual Report of the U.S. Geological Survey*, (Washington, D.C., 1896), pt. 5; *see also* Bruno Ramirez, *When Workers Fight: The Politics of Industrial Relations during the Progressive Era* (Westport, Conn.: Greenwood Press, 1978), pp. 17-29.

49. U.S. Industrial Commission, *Final Report* (Washington, D.C., Government Printing Office, 1900-1902) pp. 12, 78.

50. Quoted in Chris Evans, *History of the United Mine Workers* (Indianapolis: Hollenbeck, 1920), 1:147-50.

51. Arthur Suffern, *The Coal Miners' Struggle for Industrial Status* (New York: Macmillan, 1926), p. 40.

52. Evans, *History*, 1:275. The southern Illinois operators were willing to pay higher wages than their competition, but they would not go as high as the 95¢ a ton price set by the Joint Conference, which would have permitted their competition to pay between 65¢ and 75¢ a ton. Southern Illinois operators were not prepared to pay their employees more than 85¢ a ton. Ibid., 1:1973.

53. Ibid., p. 287; Suffern, *Coal Miners' Struggle*, p. 51.

54. Evans, *History*, 1:249-450; Suffern, *Coal Miners' Struggle*, pp. 39-43.

55. Evans, *History*, 1:275-76.

56. Ibid., pp. 278-81.

57. U.S. Industrial Commission, *Report of the Industrial Commission*

on the Relations between Labor and Capital (Washington, D.C.: Government Printing Office, 1901), 15:393.

58. *UMWJ*, December 8, 1898, p. 1; *Quincy* (Illinois) *Labor News,* July 21, 1895.

59. U.S. Industrial Commission, *Report,* 15:401. Since hard coal could not be cut by machine, the men who dug coal in eastern Pennsylvania continued to work in the traditional manner. Even as late as 1932, only 2 percent of the nation's anthracite coal was being cut by machine.

60. Carter Goodrich, *The Miners' Freedom* (New York: Workers Education Bureau of America, 1926), pp. 110-21.

61. Ibid., p. 111; John Brophy, *A Miner's Life* (Madison: University of Wisconsin Press, 1964), p. 41.

62. U.S., Industrial Commission, *Report,* 15:399; Illinois Bureau of Labor Statistics, *Annual Report, 1888* (Springfield: State Printers, 1899), pp. 339-50.

63. *UMWJ*, January 16, 1896, p. 3, April 13, 1895, p. 2.

64. Suffern, *Conciliation and Arbitration,* p. 23; *Ohio State Journal* (Columbus), June 30, 1884.

65. Quoted in *UMWJ*, November 14, 1912, p. 4.

66. Ibid., April 4, 1894, p. 4.

67. U.S. Commissioner of Labor, *Tenth Annual Report, 1894* (Washington, D.C.: Government Printing Office, 1894), pp. 452-72, 1480-84, 1668-1853.

68. *Chicago Herald* quoted in *UMWJ*, December 24, 1891, pp. 2-3.

69. *New York World,* August 25, 1889; Lloyd, *Strike of Millionaires.*

70. *See* appendix E. During these years the prices of things coal miners bought fell by only 5 percent. *See* appendix C.

71. *See* appendix F; *Indiana Union,* July 17, 1897.

72. Eliot Jones, *The Anthracite Coal Combination in the United States* (Cambridge: Harvard University Press, 1914), p. 227.

73. Ibid., p. 156.

74. Chart compiled on the basis of the data in Douglas, *Real Wages,* pp. 159-63.

75. *See* appendix G. During these years Pennsylvania's anthracite industry employed twice as many men as the state's bituminous mines. In the five years between 1890 and 1894 (unfortunately there are no available data for the later period) the average bituminous miner struck three times, while the anthracite miner struck only 0.2 times.

76. Douglas, *Real Wages,* pp. 160-63; U.S. Immigration Commission, 15:586-87.

77. "Proceedings of the Anthracite Coal Strike Commission," 1900,

Michael Koiskik Collection, Pennsylvania State University (hereafter cited as A"ACSC").

78. *Quincy* (Illinois) *Labor News,* September 29, 1900.

79. To the editor of the *Scranton Times,* September 26, 1900.

80. The Germans, English, and Irish who came to the United States during the early part of the nineteenth century are usually referred to as the old immigrants. The Russians, Slavs, and Italians, who began arriving in the United States during the last quarter of the century, were the new immigrants. U.S. Immigration Commission, 15:393; roberts, *Anthracite Coal Communities* 1.

81. Anonymous, undated letters to John Mitchell, probably written between 1895 and 1900. John Mitchell Collection, Catholic University.

82. "ACSC," 1926-1932.

83. Ibid., p. 1125.

84. Ramirez, *When Workers Fight,* p. 35; "Manuscript Census," 1900.

85. *Wilkes-Barre Record,* September 15, 1897, quoted in Victor Greene, *The Slavic Community on Strike* (Notre Dame: Notre Dame University Press, 1968) pp. 130-31.

86. For an excellent description of the anthracite coal strike of 1897, see Greene, *Slavic Community,* pp. 124-39.

87. Ibid., pp. 130-32.

88. Edward Pinkowski, *The Lattimer Massacre* (Philadelphia: University of Pennsylvania Press, 1950).

89. For an analysis of the effect of ethnic antagonisms on the UMW's organizing drive, *see* William Leiserson, *Adjusting Immigrants to Industries* (New York: Harper and Row, 1924), pp. 184-86; also *see* Michael Koiskik's fragmentary history of the United Mine Workers, Koiskik Collection.

90. *UMWJ,* March 10, 1899, p. 2.

Coal Miners on Strike

CHAPTER 3

> The day of deliverance is dawning,
> For the light of an omen we see;
> Denoting the job of the morning,
> When miners from serfdom are free.
> Never more to bow to oppression,
> Which in the past has made us feel sad,
> Beholding the day of salvation,
> Let's lift up our hearts and be glad.[1]

The bituminous coal strike of 1894 and the anthracite strikes of 1900 and 1902 repeatedly erupted in violence. Strikers usually attacked anyone who tried to cross their picket lines. Men who vowed to "eat their shirts before [going] . . . back to work as a scab" were determined to prevent strikebreakers from crossing their picket lines.[2] Since coal mine operators and government officials sought to protect any man who wanted to work, conflict was inevitable. Miners in the past had usually found state governments, many of which had enacted laws designed to keep the mines safe and well ventilated, reasonably responsive to their needs.[3] During strikes, however, the state usually became their enemy as law-enforcement officials sided with the bosses. Miners were likely to become radicalized when they found themselves in combat with militia men who tried to smash their picket lines.

On April 21, 1894, when the UMW for the first time tried to shut down the entire Central Competitive Field, the operators had responded by importing strikebreakers. The miners in turn had responded with force. Mines in Spring Valley, Illinois, and Washington Run, Pennsylvania, became immediate targets for strikers armed with dynamite. For the most part, though, violence was avoided during the early weeks of the strike as union officials maintained control. But as the strike dragged on, it became harder to keep the peace. Law-enforcement officials soon found themselves impotent because the threat of jail did not frighten the strikers. "I don't care what I do," a miner named Oscar Zamenski declared. "If I get arrested and thrown into jail, then they can send my family to the poor house, where I know they will get enough to eat."[4]

Men who felt this way would not let strikebreakers dig coal. On May 23, a month after the work stoppage began, 5,000 Illinois miners, most of whom lived in Spring Valley, organized themselves into military formation and began patrolling the Illinois coal region. The miners' first target was Centralia, where it was rumored that an operator had managed to recruit several dozen strikebreakers. Before the Spring Valley miners could find the offending operator, they were met by the county sheriff and his deputies. Seventy-five miners were arrested, but they remained in jail for only a few hours, freed by a mob of their comrades who surrounded the jail shouting, "Shall we let our brothers stay in jail?" "No, burn it down."[5]

The day after the Centralia incident, armed strikers clashed with local law-enforcement officials at nearby LaSalle. This time, fifteen hundred miners attacked a working colliery. The sheriff, after dispersing the crowd, made the mistake of arresting several of the strikers, and the miners here too marched on the city jail, threatening to burn it down unless the men were freed. At nine o'clock in the evening the frightened sheriff liberated his prisoners, but the angry crowd did not go home.[6] Instead, after an all-night rally, the miners marched to the neighboring community of Kewanee, where they forced several collieries to shut down. Ten thousand miners were now in the streets threatening to march on nearby Pana, where it was rumored that several collieries were still digging coal. Governor John Peter Altgeld, who in August was to object so eloquently when President Cleveland sent troops to Chicago to break the Pullman strike, panicked and ordered the militia into the strike zone. The governor maintained that this move was not made "to protect property, but to prevent a riot."[7]

The militia had little more effect than the local police. Enraged strikers made the soldiers targets for abuse. One miner, Henri Meisenback, backed up by a crowd, challenged a battalion of soldiers patroling LaSalle. Meisenback promised to "disembowl any soldier who tried to arrest him," another miner tried to decapitate the militia man. Meisenback and his defender were both arrested, but the militia could not keep the miners in jail. The strikers stormed the Spring Valley prison and freed the men.[8]

Although the troops did prevent the miners from invading Pana, they were unable to restore law and order. On the contrary, they probably helped escalate the violence. Realizing that they had to be mobile to elude the militia, the miners used hijacked trains to take them from one colliery to another.[9] The miner-soldier skirmishes that resulted were usually inconclusive. Finally on June 8, the militia faced a real crisis at Wesley, Illinois. That morning strikers attacked the East Little mine there that had reopened the day before. They drove the strikebreakers from the colliery and then approached it with cans of kerosene. Before the miners could light their intended bonfire, the militia arrived. The men opened fire on the troops and, as a Chicago reporter related, "Volley after volley was exchanged until the soldiers fled."[10] For a time, the strikers had the upper hand. Most operators shut down.[11]

With the collieries paralyzed, the miners turned their attention to freight trains that were carrying coal from West Virginia into the strike zone. Determined to stop this traffic in "scab coal," strike leaders rallied their following at Du Quoin, Illinois. A few hours after the meeting adjourned, several hundred strikers, accompanied by their wives and children, stopped a coal-laden train at Brazil, Indiana. The crowd detached the coal cars, leaving fifty women and children to guard them. Arming themselves with sticks and stones, the strikers' wives dared the engineer and conductor to repossess the train.[12]

Dozens of trains were so stopped, yet all coal imports could not be halted. The state militia moved quickly against any crowd that gathered near railroad tracks, forcing the miners to resort to guerrilla-type operations. The strikers and their wives began to burn railroad bridges and booby trap the tracks. Spikes, designed to derail engines, were driven between rail coupling pins.[13] Strikers, who placed ties on the tracks of the Illinois Central Railroad, told a protesting engineer that they were "determined to see to it that no coal would get through under any consideration."[14]

While most of the violence took place in Illinois, especially after the militia had been called out, there were also battles in Ohio. Here peace had reigned until late May, since almost all collieries had been shut down by the operators. The importation of West Virginia coal, however, soon shattered an uneasy calm. The Hocking Valley, through which most freight trains had to pass, became the focus of the struggle. Some of the coal trains were stopped; all were heavily stoned. When the local sheriff tried to interfere with the miners, workers' wives and children "hurried to the scene, with their aprons full of stones which they used effectively." Governor McKinley sent the militia into the strike zone, and an immediate escalation of violence occurred. The Ohio militia had no more success than their Illinois counterparts in preventing miners from dynamiting railroad cars, bridges, and stations.[15]

The violence did not end until June 12, when the leadership of the UMW, accepting an operator promise to stop reducing wages, sent the miners back to work. The union, though their men had held firm, realized that near-bankrupt operators could not reasonably be asked for increases. Even so, it had great difficulty persuading the strikers to accept the settlement. A rebellion in Ohio's Hocking Valley was controlled, but the Illinois Spring Valley miners, who had fought so hard, were more difficult to bring into line. On June 17, 12,000 of them met and adopted a resolution that demanded the resignation of the union's executive board. Ignored, they remained on the picket lines until early July, only then slowly and reluctantly returning to work.[16]

The strike was over, but its political impact remained to be felt. Before 1894, while many of its leaders were involved in radical politics, the UMW usually officially endorsed the candidates of the Democratic party. The editorial board of the *United Mine Workers Journal,* however, was controlled by the radicals, and from the beginning, they tried to convince the rank and file that the working class had to become political to "destroy monopoly."[17] On October 22, 1891, its editors analyzed the relationship of "monopoly," the "money power," and the "state." "Monopoly controls both of the old parties," they wrote. "Such being the fact, you cannot get your just share of the wealth you create unless you are in a position to force monopoly to comply with your demands." The *Journal* unequivocally asserted that "capital never has, and never will, grant anything to labor that labor is not able to force from them."[18] Populists among the leaders of the UMW saw politics as a conspiracy run by the corrupt interests in order to rob the working class of its hard-earned wealth. They believed that the workers' problems had been exacerbated by "gold bugs" who had deflated the U.S. currency by securing "the demonetization of silver in 1873," resulting in a systematic reduction of wages "until the wealth producers [could] . . . do no more than make a bare existence, while the shylock sucks the life-blood out of the nation."[19]

Many UMW leaders recognized a necessary enmity between capitalists and workers, and they tried to dramatize the class struggle to show that in such conflict the Democratic and Republican politicians were on the side of the bosses. They warned the miners that the "moneyed class would continue to rob them unless they organized economically and politically."[20] By the mid-1890s, some union leaders, moving beyond populism, began telling the miners that socialism was the only solution. W. A. Crawford, president of the UMW's Illinois district, told a group of miners assembled at Springfield that "interest, profit and taxes . . . [were] absorbing 83 percent of the wealth created, while labor receives only 17 percent."

Crawford told his audience that if they wanted a larger share of the nation's wealth, they would have to work for "government ownership, supervision and control of all sources of production."[21]

Until 1894, all such words fell on mostly deaf ears. In most elections, bituminous coal miners voted the same way as the rest of the country did. They usually gave the Republican party 55 percent of their vote and the Democratic party 45 percent. For them, as for steelworkers, ethnic and religious loyalties were the chief determinants of political behavior. Catholic coal miners tended to vote Democratic, while Protestants usually lined up behind Republican candidates. In the three decades after the Civil War, this pattern was broken only once by the violent strikes of 1876 and 1878. As it had in the Pittsburgh district, the Greenback party was able to capitalize on this class polarization and poll 20 percent of the coal town vote. Much of the Greenback vote seems to have come from voters who were normally Republican. Catholic coal miners, by and large, remained loyal to the Democratic party because the Greenbackers' support of prohibition made it impossible for many Catholics to support them.[22] At any rate, once strike memories faded, even Protestant coal miners withdrew their support from the Greenbackers and returned to the Republican party.

The decline of the Greenback party and the organization of the Populist party was hardly noticed in the coalfields. In 1892 (the Populists' best year nationally), only 2 percent of the voters who lived in the Central Competitive Field's coal towns cast ballots for General Weaver, the People's party candidate for president.[23]

In 1894, coal town politics were different. While on the picket lines, miners had discovered that the state with its militia would do almost anything in its power to defeat them. Even governors like Altgeld and McKinley, who claimed to be sympathetic, had used troops against them. This experience forced John McBride, UMW president, to break publicly with the Democratic party. His formal endorsement of the Populist cause came at a convention at Columbus, Ohio, on August 16, where he and

Illinois district president Crawford worked to cement a labor-
Populist alliance. Failing to get the AFL to endorse Populist
candidates, Crawford and several other union officials from
Ohio and Illinois ran for office themselves.[24]

The *United Mine Workers Journal* became for a time virtually
a campaign organ for the People's party. Its editors even asserted
that "independent political action [was] . . . more important than
all trade union matters combined."[25] Striking a now-familiar
line against Democrats and Republicans, they pleaded with the
miners to

> look at the legislation for the past 25 years. It has been a series of
> jobs for the benefit of the capitalist monopolies and not one act of any
> consequence for the benefit of labor. . . . It had the intended effect of
> adding billions to the wealth of those congressional clients [*sic*], every
> dollar of which has been filched from the tax paying, tax producing
> misrepresented working people. It makes no difference to us working
> people whether the Democrats or Republicans are at bat, so long as
> Wall Street controls the game.[26]

With the violence and government repression of the recent
strike so fresh in their minds, the miners responded to some
extent to their leaders and the *Journal.* In 1894, the Populist
party received 18 percent of the coal town vote in Illinois,
20 percent of the coal town vote in Ohio, and 14 percent of the
coal town vote in western and central Pennsylvania, all remarkable figures for third-party candidates. The party's lesser showing in Pennsylvania probably resulted from the fact that 30
percent of the state's soft-coal miners were recent immigrants
who could not vote. Less than 10 percent of the men who dug
coal in Illinois and Ohio, on the other hand, were not citizens.[27]
Still, even in Pennsylvania, the Populist party enjoyed significantly more support in coal towns than anywhere else in the
state. While in Ohio, Illinois, and Pennsylvania the party
received only 4 percent of the total vote, its candidates were
able to persuade 15 percent of the voters who lived in coal
towns to vote for them. Table 3.1 reproduces the election
returns.[28]

Table 3.1
1894 ELECTION IN THE COAL TOWNS OF
THE CENTRAL COMPETITIVE FIELD

State	Number of Coal Towns	Republican	Democrat	Populist	Percent Populist
Ohio	97	22,616	14,614	9,082	20
Illinois	223	28,813	18,051	8,138	18
Pennsylvania	193	26,218	12,026	6,301	14
Totals	513	77,647	44,691	23,521	15

One has to be careful about such analyses. The 1890 manuscript census was destroyed so it is impossible to determine how
many coal miners lived in these 513 coal towns.[29] The mining
population may have varied considerably from one community
to another. In some coal towns, miners and their families
probably accounted for as much as 75 percent of the population,
and in others, the mining population could have been as low as
25 percent. More importantly, we do not know how many
miners voted in 1894. It does appear, however, that the campaign generated considerable interest in coal communities,
stimulating about 70 percent of the voters who lived in such
towns to go to the polls.[30] These men were four times more likely
to vote Populist than was the population of the various states
at large.

While hardly sweeping the Central Competitive Field, the
Populists did actually carry several coal towns in 1894. Their
most significant victory came in Spring Valley, where strike
violence had reached a peak. Here the People's party received
721 of 1,294 votes cast. The Populists also did well in Ohio's
violence-ridden Hocking Valley, where they carried four coal
towns (see table 3.2).[31]

The Populists did not carry 508 coal towns, and in many,
they received less than 10 percent of the vote. Most of these
communities had remained relatively peaceful during the strike.
Thus the miners who lived in them, unlike their Spring Valley

Table 3.2
1894 ELECTION IN FOUR HOCKING VALLEY COAL TOWNS

Town	Republican	Democrat	Populist
Jacksonville	89	92	97
Sherrodsville	64	26	113
North Washington	119	36	136
Brumfield	45	91	92

and Hocking Valley counterparts, had not learned that the state was on the side of the bosses in a class struggle. Men who had not faced militia bayonets might well have believed Governors Altgeld's and McKinley's claims to be friends of the working class. Altgeld in particular had impressed many of them when he objected to President Cleveland's use of the army to break the Pullman American Railway Union strike.[32]

In 1895, the miners continued to vote Populist in about the same percentages as they had the year before. In 1896, however, the People's party fused with William Jennings Bryan's Democrats. Most coal miners, seeing no reason to vote for Bryan on the Populist line, either returned to their old parties or stopped voting. That November, voter turnout in the Central Competitive Field's 513 coal towns dropped from 70 to 46 percent.[33]

While the Populist vote was declining, the miners remained restless as the depression continued. The operators soon broke the 1894 agreement and once again reduced wages. In 1897, when the economy appeared to be recovering, the average miner, who three years earlier had been earning $1.71 a day, was earning only $1.38 a day.[34] Wildcat strikes again became frequent. On July 4, 1897, a new UMW president, M. D. Ratchford, called another suspension:

Our suspension is not a choice, . . . but it is the voice of an enslaved class urged to action by cruel and unbearable conditions, the protest of an overworked, underpaid people against longer continuing a semistarved existence. The movement is nothing less than a spontaneous uprising of an enslaved people.[35]

When reporters visited coal towns, they found that Ratchford had not exaggerated. "We could not feed and clothe our children on the wages we are getting," a man who dug coal in Indiana declared. "We are not doing much better now, but at least we are getting a vacation."[36] Others were less flippant. The wife of an Illinois miner vowed:

I'll live on bread and water and see my children live that way too, if it will help the men win. I've been trying to live and feed my young ones on an average of one dollar a week and its no use. . . . My husband has been working in the mines for the last 23 years. Part of the time he made 50¢ a day for half the month and nothing for the other half. We can't live on 25¢ a day and pay rent. We were going to starve if he kept at work, and I guess we will starve if the men lose the strike. They won't lose it if I can help it.

Another woman found herself in a similar predicament. Before the strike, she had sent her husband to work with a dinner pail that had

nothin but water in it because there was no bread after the children ate and I was doon it day after day moind ye. . . . When the four children went to school in the spraing and had to have books, we paid for them by living on two sparse meals a day, and livery day the dinner pail went down the shaft with nothin but watter in it.[37]

While striking, the miners and their families had only the produce of their small backyard gardens. This source of food could not last long. "Well we are on the verge of starvation now," one miner declared. "When our gardens are gone many of us will starve unless we get aid. We had to strike or something, what else could we do?"[38] When the gardens did run out,

starvation set in. A visitor was shocked by what he saw in the
coal towns:

Hunger has got such a hold on the miners and their wives and children
that they have lost all ambition to keep clean. The babies wallow in
the dirt of the streets and gnaw and munch sticks of grass when they
are hungry. Swarms of ragged children are beginning to forage around
the neighborhoods of the mining communities for food to keep them
and their parents from starving.[39]

It was feared that men and women living in such desperate
poverty would become violent; however, the 1897 strike turned
out to be relatively peaceful. Since most operators did not want
to see more of the kind of violence that had erupted three
years before, they did not try to reopen their collieries with
strikebreakers. By 1897, furthermore, many coal mine owners,
concluding that an industry locked in perpetual class warfare
would never be profitable, were inclined, especially with the
return of prosperity, to reach an accommodation with the UMW.

William P. Rend, one of Ohio's largest coal operators, vig-
orously pushed for such a change in policy, publicly criticizing
recalcitrant operators. He had particular scorn for Pittsburgh's
John DeArmitt. Rend told a reporter for the *Chicago Tribune* that
"DeArmitt starves his men until they lose respect for law and
order and in their wild frenzy to avenge their wrongs and secure
bread for their starving families, they bare their breasts to the
bayonets of the state militia." Pointing an accusing finger at the
Pittsburgh coal baron, Rend asked rhetorically:

Who is the worst enemy of society? The selfless man who is led to teach
others lawlessness through a misguided enthusiasm, or the cold
blooded scoundrel who, hiding behind a mask of hypocrisy, drives
thousands to desperation by oppression and starvation wages.[40]

Claiming that DeArmitt's wage cutting had forced the miners
to strike, Rend asserted that "all responsible coal mine operators"

were willing to arbitrate their differences with the UMW. These men believed that their businesses were threatened by something far more ominous than the possibility of having to pay the men who worked for them an additional few cents a day for digging coal:

I want the strike to end on any equitable and fair terms, and I am willing to take the chance of financial loss [Rend declared]. I have no conditions to impose and I am willing to agree to anything which will end the trouble and avert bloodshed and violence which is sure to come sooner or later. The strike now menaces all business interests and if prolonged will surely endanger public peace. If the struggle is prolonged hunger and despair may incite the strikers to violence. The men are entitled to a living wage. When a laborer is paid less, neither argument nor philosophy will resolve him to accept his lot.[41]

By 1897, most bituminous coal mine operators appear to have come to share Rend's outlook. Most of them kept to their resolve not to import strikebreakers. There were a few irreconcilables, of course, who caused trouble to erupt at Danville, Coffeen, and Roanoke, Illinois. Such outbreaks, with their evident cause, confirmed the overall desire for peace on both sides.[42]

John DeArmitt got the trouble he had been asking for. His efforts to dig coal were thwarted by militant picket lines. When the governor of Pennsylvania refused militia protection, DeArmitt's mines remained closed. On July 31, nevertheless, the Pittsburgh coal baron managed to get a handful of strikebreakers into a colliery. Eight hundred strikers immediately marched to the mine where they were met by an equal number of previously alerted deputy sheriffs. A few gunshots were exchanged, and twelve strikers were arrested and taken to a detention center at nearby Turtle Creek. At that juncture, Pat Dolan, UMW vice-president, arrived with Eugene Debs, who had been working with the union during the strike. The two men persuaded the miners to retreat. The crowd pulled back but did not go home. Instead, determined to free their comrades, the strikers marched toward Turtle Creek. Debs was again there to meet the crowd. He did his best to convince the strikers not to take the law into their own hands, treating the miners instead to a blistering attack on the capitalist system. He asked the strikers:

What is the difference between the American workingman and the Russian serf? There in Russia is one Tsar and here there are a thousand. In no country on the face of the earth is the average workingman so much the tool of his master as in the land of the free.[43]

The miners cheered Debs's every sentence, but his words dissolved the tension. The arrested miners remained in the makeshift jail.

John DeArmitt, evidently shaken by the near revolt, again closed his collieries, at least for a time. When he tried to reopen on August 24, he was again stymied by 500 men and women who surrounded his scabs and forced them to "flee over the hills, leaving their dinner pails behind."[44] Even DeArmitt then saw the need to compromise with the UMW. His favorite tactic of threatening less-resolute operators with sales of cheap scab coal had no hope against miners resolved to prevent any coal at all from being dug.[45]

On September 8, 1897, the strike ended. The UMW gained recognition as the bargaining agent for the Central Competitive Field's soft-coal miners, wages were raised by 20 percent, and both labor and management promised to settle all their differences in the future by collective bargaining. Thus the reestablishment of the Joint Conference system under the agreement finally brought peace to the bituminous coalfields. The return of prosperity in 1898 gave the system some chance of lasting.

Nevertheless, the 1897 strike once again led to a resurgence of Populist sentiment. In the 1898 gubernatorial elections in Pennsylvania and Ohio, the Populist party received 13 percent of the coal town vote.[46] There were other straws in the wind. The increasingly radical Eugene Debs, though not running for office in 1898, received a warm reception during an Illinois speaking tour. Wherever Debs spoke in the coalfields, it appeared as if whole towns came out to listen to him. Miners, their wives, and their children were anxious to shake his hand, not infrequently presenting him with a bouquet of flowers.

At Spring Valley, Debs rented the large Opera House, but not more than one-quarter of the crowd could get in. So after speaking indoors, Debs went to the school park to address the throng that had assembled there. The meeting produced thirty-four miners who were able to afford to pay dues and join the young Social Democratic party. At Coal City, "notwithstanding a heavy rain," a Socialist paper reported, "many came from miles around to hear." There Debs managed to persuade eighty-six men to join the Socialist party. At Carbondale, Braidwood, Coffeen, Pana, and Virden, Debs was mobbed by thousands delighted by his denunciations of the capitalist system.[47]

Pana and Virden were towns where socialism was to have a lasting impact. Debs's oratory doubtless helped, but labor-management conflict had more to do with the Socialists' relative success in these two tiny coal communities. In the winter of 1898, Joint Conference operators sold their collieries to a group of men who were determined to break the union. In the spring the new owners organized the Chicago-Virden Coal Company. Preparing for battle, they evicted the miners from company-owned houses and built stockades around the collieries. A lockout began on April 11, 1898. There was no serious trouble until August when the operators began to import black strikebreakers from Alabama. On September 1, a miners' meeting decided to march on the mines "to take the negroes out." Just then, John Mitchell, president of the UMW's Illinois district, arrived in town and managed to calm the miners. The men, however, did not long keep their promise to Mitchell to refrain from violence. The next day, thirty of them surrounded the Pana sheriff and two foremen who were sitting on the porch of the Hotel de Pana. The miners forced the three prisoners to march to the collieries. Once there, the captives were instructed to bring the strikebreakers to the surface. When they refused, violence again threatened, but John Mitchell once again arrived.[48]

Mitchell was able to keep the peace that day and for several more weeks. On September 30, however, the operators tried to bring an even larger group of strikebreakers into the mines. The UMW could no longer control the miners. A trainload of black strikebreakers was prevented from stopping at the Pana railroad station.[49] The police moved on the strikers. After a violent battle, Governor John Tanner ordered in the state militia. The governor acted, however, for the unprecedented purpose of keeping the Chicago-Virden Coal Company from importing strikebreakers, forcing the coal mine owners not only to end the strike but to agree to pay union scale.[50]

The agreement did not last long. In the spring of 1899 when the operators decided to cut wages, the miners struck. The Alabama blacks were the only men who crossed the picket lines. The miners resorted to terror to drive the strikebreakers from the town. Again the militia was summoned to the strike zone, but this time the troops were unable to restore order. The local commander disregarded Governor Tanner's renewed instructions to the contrary and ordered armed escorts for the strikebreakers.[51] The governor ignored this infraction of his own orders, and it appeared as if the strike might be broken. During May and June, the soldiers were in complete control. In July, though, the miners rallied. On July 9, the troops stood by helplessly while the miners drove 450 strikebreakers out of town at gunpoint. The operators were once again forced to promise to pay union scale.[52]

During the Pana-Virden mine wars, the Illinois Social Democratic party managed to make its presence felt. On September 30, 1898, G. A. Hoelin, the party's state secretary, told victims of the first lockout, "The monopolists have been trying to suppress you and starve your children. Gatling guns for starving workmen. Shame upon the capitalist system that has nothing but hot lead for its best citizens."[53] This message was echoed by Eugene Debs who asked the embattled miners to "help sweep the competitive system with its Homesteads and Panas out of existence."[54]

More than a year after the second strike, Debs again visited Pana, this time asking the miners to vote for him in the presidential election of 1900. Two weeks later when the citizens of Pana and Virden went to the polls, 353 of the towns' 905 voters cast ballots for socialism.[55] Debs and his fellow Socialists, however, did poorly in coal towns that had remained peaceful after the 1897 settlement. Spring Valley, where Debs was named on 189 of 1,456 ballots, was the only other mining community in the Central Competitive Field to give him more than 10 percent of its vote.[56] The Pana-Virden mine wars clearly showed that embattled miners, for whom the class struggle had become a reality, would respond to the Socialist message. This lesson was to be put to good use by the party during the 1902 anthracite coal strike.

Until the late 1890s, the UMW was so preoccupied with the bituminous coalfields that it made almost no effort to organize the anthracite coal miners. The successful 1897 strike in the Central Competitive Field gave the union the chance to work in eastern Pennsylvania, and its efforts were rewarded almost immediately. By the summer of 1899, 45,000 men, representing one-third of the anthracite coal miners, had joined the union.

Like their bituminous counterparts of a decade before, the new unionists were eager for a showdown. Rank-and-file militancy gave union officials much trouble. The leadership still felt compelled to conserve the union's strength by avoiding strikes, but sometimes it lost control. In March and April 1899, there were strikes involving more than 10,000 miners at Pittston, Duryea, and Nanticoke. The Nanticoke conflict, which lasted more than eight months, resulted in frequent clashes between miners and law-enforcement authorities.[57]

Even so, the *United Mine Workers Journal* pleaded for patience. "It should be the object of every union man to resolutely refuse to be led into these traps," the editors advised in April 1900. "Let us hold the organization we have during the next few months, increase it as much as possible, and then, in July, demand from the operators an adjustment, and if they refuse, then strike."[58] Such pleas did little good. Early in June, T. D. Nicolls, the harassed president of District 1, informed UMW President John Mitchell that "a majority of the men in our district want to strike, and we have actually got to fight them and show them the folly of small strikes. Then many of them leave the union, because they cannot strike. . . . Our only salvation is a decisive move at an early date."[59] Union officials ran from colliery to colliery begging the miners to stay on the job a few weeks longer, but their efforts were in vain. In June, there were strikes in Yatesville, Wilkes-Barre, Archibald, and Old Forge. According to Nicolls more were "threatening." The angry president of District 1 complained that these strikes were "illegally declared by men who have borne their grievances for years, but as soon as they are organized they expect redress right away."[60]

An industry-wide suspension for anthracite could be postponed no longer. Further delay might alienate the miners from the UMW. On August 16, 1900, John Mitchell called the presidents of the region's local unions together to plan strike action. The convention drew up a list of complaints against the operators: falling wages, oversized mine cars that required 3,360 pounds to make a ton, arbitrary foremen, long hours, and unsafe mines. The convention demanded that the operators increase wages by 20 percent and recognize the UMW as the bargaining agent. The operators were invited to a Joint Conference, but only G. M. Cummings, vice-president of the Erie Railroad, expressed any interest in such an idea.[61]

The walkout began on September 17, 1900. The response to the strike call surprised even the most optimistic union men. On September 17, between 80,000 and 100,000 men did not report for work. A week later, 125,000 miners were striking, and by September 26, 142,000 of the 152,000 men who dug anthracite coal were on the picket lines.[62] As in the bituminous region six years before, the militancy of the miners promised success for the strike. Men, long clearly willing to use force to keep the mines closed, could make a strike effective.

Such force had to be used at once in the Wilkes-Barre-Scranton region, the scene of the 1897 work stoppage. Here an unusually large number of English-speaking miners, who wanted to keep working, tempted the operators to try to keep their mines open. The strikers quickly marched from mine to mine, forcing most of the collieries to close. They met real resistance, however, at the Coxe brothers' mine on the outskirts of Wilkes-Barre. There a sheriff and his deputies tried to stand fast. The sheriff screamed, "This is an outrage. You have come to terrorize a peaceful community." His anger only enraged the crowd. One man shouted back at him, "There has been no breach of the peace. You are not needed here, you are not wanted. . . . You do not represent the state of the country, you are a hireling of a corporation, armed by a corporation to defend its property." Inspired by so doughty a spokesman, the cheering miners pushed by the sheriff and closed down the mine.[63]

Violence next threatened to erupt in Shenandoah, where most of the mines had also tried to remain open. At a strategy session held on September 20, the miners organized themselves into "flying squadrons" to intercept mine-bound workers. The next day, they stopped trolley cars and searched for suspected strikebreakers. Then they moved on to the collieries and drove out any strikebreakers who had managed to get to work. When the sheriff tried to escort the evicted scabs to safety, several hundred men began to pelt him with eggs and stones. One deputy described the scene: "The Poles came out of their quarters as thick as flies, backed up and fought! When the officers finally did get through the mob, they were throwing things at us from all the houses, crockery, beer bottles, anything." The frightened police opened fire, killing one man and seriously wounding seven others.[64]

Ethnic differences gave the violence at Shenandoah a savage edge. It became a battle between the "foreigners" and the "natives," so much so that many English-speaking union men volunteered their services to the sheriff. One said, "I am a miner and so are most of the posse. We are all good citizens and we will protect the town with our lives if we have to." This man maintained that he was not against the strike. "We hope to win the strike," he declared, "but rioting will not. These fellows are ignorant. Many have not been in this country more than six months and we cannot talk to them. They don't understand anything about a strike."[65] Such sentiments were deeply felt by much of the English-speaking population of Shenandoah. The miner turned deputy and his friends were convinced that "anarchists . . . [had] seized control of the situation to precipitate a riot." They disclaimed any desire to help the "railroads open the collieries, but . . . [promised to] protect the town and its citizens." When English-speaking miner deputies began to patrol Slavic and Italian neighborhoods, there were bloody clashes.[66]

On September 25, Governor George Stone ordered the militia to Shenandoah. General William Gobin, with 2,200 armed men, restored order without too much difficulty. Two weeks later, the governor felt safe in withdrawing the troops, but with the militia gone, violence quickly erupted again.

More weeks of strike throughout the region brought further efforts at mine reopenings amid heightened tension. Several collieries in the Wilkes-Barre-Scranton region did open on October 15 but were immediately surrounded by groups of militant pickets totaling some 3,000. Even Mother (Mary Harris) Jones, who at seventy years still managed to be, perhaps, the union's most militant organizer, feared the mounting violence. Jones, who in the past had encouraged beatings of strikebreakers and attacks on police and militia, now had words of caution: "Men on strike are at a terrible nervous tension. They must give vent to their feelings. Leave them alone [unguided] and they will do murder in their mad, misguided excitement."[67]

The leaders of the UMW shared Mother Jones's fears. Dozens of them came to the region begging the miners to keep calm. In an effort to control the hungry men and women, they tried the distraction of organizing marches and rallies. One union official asserted, "I am a safety valve for this strike. I lead the men on long marches over the mountains to work off their surplus energy.[68] Such tactics kept the peace for a while, but as more and more mines reopened, the situation threatened to explode. Then the National Civic Federation and its first president, Marcus Alonzo Hanna, intervened.

Mark Hanna, a one-time coal and iron baron and now a full-time politician, was alarmed by the spectacle of armed miners parading around eastern Pennsylvania. He was convinced that the operators' uncompromising position would result in further violence. Even early in the strike he had been quoted by the *Scranton Times* as saying:

Any man who would put a straw in the way of a settlement should be strung up to a lamppost. The greater part of the miners have not enough money to last them more than a month. A continuation of the strike would mean accordingly want and hunger, and when men are hungry they are desperate. Bloodshed and rioting would result and that would be a calamity for the whole country.[69]

Hanna the politician was sensitive to the political implications of continued unrest in the anthracite coalfields. He knew that another coal strike would radicalize the miners and destroy any hopes that the Republican party had for carrying the region. In fact, since almost half of the anthracite coal miners were Catholic, the Republican party usually did not do as well in eastern Pennsylvania as it did in the western part of the state. In most elections, anthracite coal towns were evenly split between Republicans and Democrats. Some years Democrats won majorities; other years the Republicans were triumphant.[70]

As in the bituminous coalfields, strikes and class conflict usually helped the cause of radical third parties. The so-called long strike of 1875 and the shorter but more violent strike of 1877, which were fought against the background of the Molly Maguire insurrection, polarized the anthracite coal region along class lines, enabling the Greenback party to capture more than 50 percent of the coal town vote. The Greenback party owed much of its success to the fact that in the anthracite region, class polarization was intense enough to transcend ethnic and religious divisions. Here Catholic coal miners were just as likely to vote for the Greenback ticket as were their Protestant neighbors. In eastern Pennsylvania prohibition was less important than class. But again once the strike wounds healed, the Democrats and Republicans reasserted their traditional hegemony. This pattern remained unbroken until the 1897 Wyoming Valley strike enabled the Populist party to capture 25 percent of the coal town vote. In areas where strike violence was particularly intense, the Populist vote approached 60 percent, but when the People's party collapsed in 1898, the Democrats and Republicans were again supreme.[71]

Sobered by this history, Mark Hanna desperately sought a labor-management peace that would strengthen the UMW's conservative leadership. In 1900, the fledgling Socialist party was not yet strong enough to have an impact, but Hanna looked to the future with trepidation. The coal mine operators, however, remained unmoved. Unlike their bituminous counterparts, they did not need the union to stabilize competitive market conditions, so they were determined to fight the UMW to the end. Therefore, for the moment, Hanna could win only a truce that gave the miners a 10 percent increase.[72]

The truce was uneasy. As soon as it was signed, both the UMW and the operators began preparing for the next conflict. Foremen and superintendents, determined to destroy the union, began to put the names of active union men on blacklists, and militant miners were dismissed. Operators began to hire private armies of Coal and Iron Police, recently authorized by the state, to guard the collieries. Stockades were built around more collieries so that the troops would be able to defend them when the showdown came.[73]

The UMW also made ready. It worked feverishly to sign up the more than 90,000 miners who, however willing to strike, had remained outside the union. Organizers visited every mining town in the region, telling all who would listen that the operators would never improve conditions until the UMW commanded the loyalties of all the miners. The union's efforts were quite successful. By the winter of 1901, more than 100,000 anthracite coal miners had joined, reducing the number of holdouts to about 50,000.

John Mitchell hoped that 100,000 dues-paying miners would force the operators to sit down and negotiate peacefully. On February 8, 1901, he requested such negotiations. Striking an accommodating tone, he emphasized the advantages the Joint Conference had brought to the bituminous coal miners and promised that union recognition would guarantee labor peace. "It appears to me," he told the owners, "that it must be obvious to you, that the miners' organization is a responsible institution conducted on conservative business lines."[74]

The miners themselves were not so conciliatory. After the 1900 strike had ended, foremen and superintendents had found it difficult to manage the many men who had been left dissatisfied by the settlement. "Why it used to be before the 1900 strike," one of them declared, "that if I set men to work or laid out work at night to be done in the morning and got it under way that I could leave it, but since then I have found that it would be left in the morning and I would have to stay there and get it done myself." When told to clean windows or sweep floors, miners would often snarl, "taint none of my business." Foremen, who insisted on such duties, were told, "I won't and if you fire me I'll call out the other fellows." Such threats were made good. One foreman had a strike after he reprimanded a mule driver for leaving his animal without food for three days.[75]

Such complaints from foremen and superintendents might be suspect, but an observer from labor's side confirmed them. The journalist, Walter Weyl, was a close friend of, and sometimes ghost writer for, John Mitchell.[76] In an article under his own byline in the July 1902 *Outlook,* he observed that "in some mines matters [had] . . . reached such a crisis that foremen were afraid to address men either in reproach or with advice, while to issue a command was to court a gratuitous insult."[77] The men in some mines became so rancorous against both foremen and union officials that they struck every other month. In the summer of 1901, the entire northern field near Scranton was paralyzed, and slowdowns reduced productivity in those mines that could work by 25 percent.[78] The union's conservative leadership continued its pleas for patience but to little avail. One frustrated organizer wrote John Mitchell that a union that could no longer control its men "was going down hill almost as fast as it was raised."[79]

The operators seemed oblivious to the crisis. Even J. P. Morgan, whose syndicates owned most of the stock in the anthracite railroads, found it impossible to persuade the railroad presidents to accept the UMW. Threatening to resign if Morgan persisted in pressuring them, the railroad presidents asserted that they would rather go into bankruptcy than recognize the union. They spurned Mitchell's every overture.[80] A showdown became inevitable.

Local union officials, beleaguered by their men, finally forced John Mitchell to call a convention once again to plan strike action. When the delegates assembled at Hazleton, Pennsylvania, on May 14, 1902, Mitchell said bluntly, "We can work out our problems by the methods we are now pursuing."[81] But local leaders left their president no choice but to call a strike. A few days later he explained what had happened at the convention to his friends and fellow National Civic Federationist, Mark Hanna:

I was hopeful that the anthracite strike would be averted or at least delayed and I used all the power at my command to bring this about, but it developed in the Hazleton convention that our delegates were almost unanimous in their determination to enforce concessions.[82]

On May 16, 1902, the strike began. This time the conflict between the militia and the strikers was far more intense than it had been two years before. The miners and their families were no longer intimidated by the mere presence of the troops. Only by overt force could the soldiers protect the collieries. The battles that resulted were class conflict of a kind that most Marxists had long believed would convert any proletariat to socialism.

The strike from the start looked like a fight to the finish. "When the strike was about to be declared," one coal town minister said later, "a company of foreigners visited a mining town to purchase arms. They shouted 'ye strike' all over town and the prudent man picked up his tools and went home. On each road an organized troop was posted and if any employee came to work that morning there would have been trouble.[83] Outnumbered, sheriffs and their deputies could not protect the collieries. As in previous strikes, mines were shot up, shafts were dynamited, and pumping stations and company stores were put to the torch.[84] Women joined their husbands and sons on the picket lines. Armed with pots, pans, and rolling pins, they yielded to nobody in their militancy. Their scorn against strikebreakers was merciless. If that did not work, they used stones and clubs.[85] Any supervisor or miner who tried to work became a prime target. The houses of such men were often destroyed and their lives theatened.[86] Many of them were beaten, and a few were killed.[87]

The UMW leadership did its best to keep the peace. The union officials did not want to give Governor Stone another excuse to call out the militia, so they begged the miners to "above everything else refrain from violence. Keep away from the collieries and do nothing to warrant the calling out of the militia."[88] For the most part, the strikers now had enough confidence in their leaders to listen. However, when promised strike relief did not arrive, even union leaders found themselves in danger. George Hartlein, the president of a Scranton local union, had a real scare on at least one occasion. In a letter to John Mitchell he vividly described the scene:

They are mostly foreigners, the committee said there was hell to pay for an hour before I got there, every person was talking at once, but when I got into the room you could have heard a pin drop, but ye Gods in looking in the men's eyes it would have taken a pretty strong man not to have trembled, and I will say if I had known things as they were I would have never attempted to go in there alone. . . . My heart was in my throat. . . . I had to keep swallowing often to keep it down at the right place. I told them that they were the easiest led bunch of people it had ever been for my time to meet and if they did not have respect for themselves, at least respect their leader, John Mitchell.

As soon as Hartlein mentioned the name John Mitchell, the local union leader claimed, the tone of the meeting changed. The crowd calmed down and listened to what he had to say. "After I was finished they gave three cheers for John Mitchell and voted to stand there with him through thick and thin."[89]

During the first two and a half months of the strike, violence was mostly sporadic, amounting at most to property damage and intimidation. The July 29 battle of Shenandoah changed everything. The use of English-speaking strikebreakers precipitated the conflict, and, as usual, it was Slavic and Italian immigrants who responded militantly. The battle began when superintendent David Lederman, his son, and a dozen scabs who had been camping behind the Kohinoor Coal Company's stockade tried to return home. Wearing women's clothing, they tried to sneak out from behind the fortification, but almost immediately they were recognized. When surrounded by the strikers, Lederman drew his revolver and began to fire wildly at the crowd. His gun was silenced by a shotgun blast. The superintendent, his son, and the strikebreakers, though all were seriously wounded, were beaten before they were allowed to stagger off.[90]

The next evening tension reached a climax. Angry Shenandoah miners encountered deputy sheriff Thomas Bedall escorting three strikebreakers home from the Indian Ridge colliery. The crowd jumped them. Bedall opened fire, but this only brought more strikers to the scene. The deputy and the strikebreakers barely managed to escape to a nearby store where they barricaded themselves inside. By now, there were 5,000 men and women in the streets, screaming for Bedall's blood. The deputy's brother-in-law tried to elbow his way through the crowd, but he was spotted, accused of carrying ammunition, and beaten to death. The police moved in, but their gunfire did not intimidate the miners and their families. John Fahy, president of the union's District 9, arrived on the scene at the same time the police did. He called upon the miners "to suppress lawlessness, and to aid the officers in every way," but his voice could not be heard above the roar of the crowd.[91]

The governor, hearing of the riot, decided that the militia, on standby alert, had to be sent to Shenandoah. Once again, General Gobin and his troops marched into town. The soldiers with their superior firepower were able to force the crowd to disperse, but the strikers went home enraged by the militia's brutality. The UMW could no longer control the miners, nor could the soldiers.

Pennsylvania's adjutant general, William V. Miller, saw the problem clearly: "There are not 50,000 soldiers in existence today who can patrol every colliery, every home, and every road in a district as large as the anthracite region of Eastern Pennsylvania," he observed.[92] After two months of active duty, even General Gobin was forced to report his failure to Governor Stone. "There is such a species of intimidation," his report read, "that although I have very excellent secret service men, and my officers are as diligent as officers could be, there are so many things to be done that I cannot do them all at once."[93]

The militia could not cope with 150,000 strikers, many of whom had the active aid of families and friends. One day at Gilberton, trolley cars were stopped and searched for strikebreakers. The next day several thousand men and women stormed the Pottsville jail, freeing the prisoners that had been

taken in the Shenandoah riot. At other times bridges were dynamited, collieries were burned, and railroad trains destroyed.[94]
No matter how fast the militia moved, it could not keep up.

Leaders of the UMW kept trying to restore peace. Sometimes
law-enforcement officials cooperated with the union, but
usually just when the situation was most critical, they preferred
to ignore the union and call in the militia. Thomas Greenley,
president of the union's Shenandoah local, believed he could
have prevented the riot there had local authorities cooperated
with him, as the sheriff had promised. The town's mayor had
promised to keep Coal and Iron Police out of the city. But after
the incident at the Kohinoor mine, the superintendent of
the nearby Indian Ridge colliery hired seventy-five armed
men to protect his strikebreakers. Greenley had managed
to keep his men in check; then he had rushed to city hall to
see the mayor and the police chief. He assured them that if
they would "get rid of the Coal and Iron Police and not
send anyone in . . . the union would appoint a local committee
and there would be no disturbance."[95] The mayor, however, had
refused, ordering Deputy Bedall instead to see that the
strikebreakers got home safely. It was Bedall's effort that
brought on the Shenandoah riot.

So it had been, too, with the soldiers brought in to put
down the riot. General Gobin's frustrations led him to issue a
shoot-to-kill order. His troops were instructed to fire on anyone
who failed to respond to their orders. When escorting strikebreakers through picket lines, the soldiers shot or clubbed all
who interfered. Strikers who two years before had not been
hostile to the militia naturally saw the troops as their enemies.

Such indiscriminate violence from their government gave
quite a few miners radical ideas. The presidents of the anthracite railroads remained unperturbed, but Mark Hanna and the
NCF again became worried. Ralph Easley, the organization's
executive secretary, asserted that

it is important for the industrial development of this country to have
the strike settled. The only ones who profit by its continuance are the
radical element, composed of Socialists and Populists, who are fighting

capitalism at every turn, using every effort to create class prejudice.
The strongest natural ally that the community of interests idea has today
is organized labor. I know the operators, who believe that they have the
God given right to operate the mines, won't appreciate this.[96]

Even so, all the efforts of Easley and Hanna seemed unavail-
ing. They could not convince the railroad presidents of Hanna's
belief that by alliance "with responsible trade unionists, they
would not only gain a peaceful labor situation but a ready and
willing ally in the fight against Socialism."[97]

Failing to budge the operators, the NCF, joined by many
conservative Republican senators and congressmen, urged
President Theodore Roosevelt to threaten the presidents of the
anthracite railroads with seizure of their collieries. On October
6, Senator Henry Cabot Lodge of Massachusetts, Roosevelt's
close friend and adviser, told the president that

it is difficult to consider with calmness the attitude of the operators.
Anything worse or more foolish than the manner in which they are
behaving is difficult to conceive. They are not only causing great
suffering and probably the defeat of the Republican party, but their
attitude is a menace to all prosperity in the country and is breeding
Socialism at a rate which is hard to contemplate.[98]

A few days after receiving Lodge's letter, Roosevelt summoned Mitchell and the presidents of the anthracite railroads to
Washington, but failed to persuade either to compromise. The
operators would not recognize the UMW, and Mitchell, though
conciliatory on all other issues, would settle for nothing less.
Undiscouraged, Roosevelt continued to work behind the scenes.
Eventually both the miners and the operators agreed to seek a
settlement through a presidential commission. On October 23,
1902, the miners returned to work.[99]

After months of hearings, the Anthracite Coal Strike Commission made strong recommendations to the president. Its final
report set the rules that were to govern labor-management
relations in the industry for a generation. In the interest of
compromise, the commission recommended a nine-hour day

rather than one of eight that had been demanded by the
union and a 10 percent increase in wages instead of 20 percent.
The commission did not exact formal recognition for the
UMW, but after 1903, the union was treated as if it were the
miners' bargaining agent.[100]

The compromise, nevertheless, did not keep the NCF's night-
mare about socialism from almost becoming a reality. During
and immediately after the strike, many miners became involved
in radical politics. A Wilkes-Barre miner pleaded with John
Mitchell for guidance in this struggle:

It looks as tho the rich people and the citizens alliances all over the
country and the deplorable Republican authorities of the law in the
state, county and municipalities, elected by the poor laboring class are
ready to cut off our heads and put us in prison as soon as we look for our
rights. They are all against us. As General Gobin said the other day that
if necessary he would send a Gatling gun to mow us poor United
Mine Workers down. He is trying to please the rich coal barons and
make himself a great man in their eyes, and make slaves of us once
more for them to crush all the wealth possible out of us. . . . But I hope
you will do all in your power to put this terrible strike to an end and if it
lasts until election time in November, give us a hint of how to vote for
the right man or right party. . . . We can get nowhere with the demons
and hypocrites of the Republicans and Democrats. . . . We need the
right man who will do something for us. Cast the hypocrites and
cowards, and parasites aside for ever, for they have deceived us for
many, many years, and have never done anything for us. They thought
we were geese. It is time for us to open our eyes and be geese no more.[101]

Such pleas were unlikely to shake Mitchell's lifetime political
loyalties. In fact, during the 1902 election campaign, he worked
cheerfully with his fellow National Civic Federationist, Mark
Hanna, assuring the Republican boss of his wish to contain "the
great independent political sentiment . . . created by . . . the
brutal order of General Gobin . . . known as his 'shoot to kill
order.' "[102]

Predictably, the Socialist party was more responsive than
John Mitchell to class exploitation and repression. It had gone to
work in the anthracite region as soon as the strike began. Some

organizers handed out leaflets and held rallies, and others distributed almost $10,000 in needed strike relief.[103] No Socialist had to tell the embattled miners that they were engaged in a class struggle. Party people, however, did try to make clear the role of the state and its politicians in the conflict in ways that John Mitchell would only acknowledge in private correspondence. "The capitalists are the power of the government," they declared. "Government makes laws for their benefit and sets judges on the bench to issue injunctions against you and employs police and militia to enforce the laws and if need be to put you in prison or shoot you down."[104]

The Socialists tried to convince the miners that they were working for starvation wages because "the capitalist class controls the politics of our country. When you strike they call out the militia to shoot you down."[105] The Socialists pointed out how advantageous it would be for the miners to have the power of the state on their side in the class struggle. "Now if the power of government is so useful to the capitalists, why should it not be equally useful to you? If it is used to make slaves of you, why should it not be used to set you free?"[106]

In order to show what socialism could mean for the men who dug coal, the Socialists tried to explain Marx's theory of surplus value to the miners:

The joint labor of myriads of men [one leaflet read] creates everything of value in the mine and the breaker and the coal roads, and yet, this handful of useless capitalists control the whole industry for their profit. Consider you miners now on strike for excessively moderate demands. . . . For these very small demands you have to endure the suffering of a strike. Yet, you have the right to more than double the amount you are now receiving in wages. Your labor produces more than twice as much as you get back. The larger half goes to Morgan and his friends. Under Socialism you would get all you produce.[107]

The length and violence of the strike eventually brought the Socialists real response. Each of the party's four full-time organizers in the area found himself establishing at least one local a day. Over a period of a few months, the average membership of these locals increased from 25 to 340.[108] Organizer William Mailley was overwhelmed by the response. "I have never seen men who listened with such unfeigned enthusiasm to the Socialist presentation as these men," he wrote while the strike was at its height. He proudly proclaimed that "Socialist meetings, exceeding in size and enthusiasm any political meetings, are now being held at all points where we have speakers."[109] Even party people were surprised to discover that "Socialism [was being] . . . discussed as much, if not more, than the strike." Their only regret was they did not have "enough literature to distribute among the eager miners."[110]

As the 1902 Pennsylvania gubernatorial election drew near, the Socialists realized that they were going to do very well in the eastern parts of the state. A comrade, Fisher, who was working in Luzerne County, begged the party's national office for six more English-speaking and two Polish-speaking organizers to "insure victory."[111] The more I study the attitude of the masses to the Socialist party of Luzerne, "he declared, "the more I am convinced that they will come out in a compact body for Socialism.[112]

In November, the party's candidate for governor, John W. Slayton, did well in eastern Pennsylvania. With 76 percent of the eligible voters who lived in the region's 255 coal towns going to the polls, the Socialists received 24 percent of the vote.[113]

It was an impressive turnout, particularly when compared to the 0.3 percent of the vote that Slayton received throughout Pennsylvania that year or the 1 percent of the presidential vote that candidate Eugene Debs had received in these coal towns two years earlier. The Socialists might have done even better had they not had to run against a reform-minded, Anti-Machine party in Lackawanna County. Made up largely of dissident Democrats, this splinter group appears to have wooed many English-speaking miners by its strong criticism of the militia.[114]

Lackawanna County's ethnic composition was at least partially responsible for the success of the Anti-Machine party. While more than 75 percent of the coal miners who lived in Carbon, Northcumberland, Luzerne, and Schuylkill counties were of Italian or Slavic descent, 65 percent of Lackawanna's coal miners were native born or of Irish and Scottish origin. These English-speaking miners were much less likely to vote Socialist than were their Slavic and Italian counterparts.[115] As table 3.3 shows, the Socialists received only 14 percent of the vote in Lacka-wanna County, while they got almost 30 percent of the vote in Carbon, Luzerne, Northcumberland, and Schuylkill counties. Given but a portion of the Anti-Machine vote, they might well have outvoted the Republicans in Lackawanna, as they did in Carbon County.

The Socialists were further handicapped by the fact that approximately 75 percent of the coal town residents were recent immigrants who did not yet qualify for citizenship. The men whose militancy made a Socialist vote likely were disenfranchised. Nevertheless, table 3.3 shows that despite these handicaps, John W. Slayton, the party's candidate for governor, captured nearly 25 percent of the anthracite coal region's vote.[116]

Table 3.3
1902 ELECTION IN 255 ANTHRACITE COAL TOWNS

County	Number of Coal Towns	Republican	Democrat	Socialist	Anti-Machine
Carbon	22	719	919	899	
Lackawanna	47	1,168	2,302	817	2,483
Luzerne	95	3,419	4,062	2,853	
Northcumberland	32	2,452	2,484	2,363	
Schuylkill	59	4,138	7,366	2,904	
Total	255	11,896	17,133	9,836	2,483

Again, as in the bituminous coalfields, the Socialists did particularly well in towns that had experienced violence. The party got more than 40 percent of the vote in Shenandoah, Mahonoy City, Nanticoke, Duryea, and Lansford; it received a majority of the votes in Garfield, Marshallton, Sagmon, Springfield, and Uniontown; and its candidates won pluralities in Maunch

Chunk, Audenreid, and Parkview.[117] In these coal towns
political radicalism was a result of heightened class conflict
associated with the strike. Would it last? Were the miners
permanently wedded to socialism, or, when the strike wounds
healed, would Socialist sentiment evaporate?

NOTES

1. George Korson, *Coal Dust on the Fiddle: Songs and Stories of the
Bituminous Coal Industry* (Philadelphia: University of Pennsylvania
Press, 1943), p. 409.

2. Quoted in Charles B. Spahr, "The Miners Strike: Some Impressions in the Field," *Outlook*, May 31, 1902, p. 89.

3. As early as the mid-1870s lobbyists representing the miners had
convinced many state legislatures to appoint mine inspectors to ensure
that the collieries were safe and well ventilated. Some states even
appointed officials of the National Federation of Miners and Mine
Laborers to these positions. Andrew Roy, the union's secretary, was a
mine inspector in Ohio for much of the 1880s. Harold Aurland, *From
Molly Maguires to the United Mine Workers* (Philadelphia:University of
Pennsylvania Press, 1971), p. 73; Katherine A. Harvey, *The Best Dressed
Miners: Life and Labor in Maryland Coal Region* (Ithaca: Cornell University Press, 1969), p. 207.

4. *Chicago Tribune*, April 27, 28, May 1, 1894. Much of what
follows is based on articles that appeared in the *Chicago Tribune*. Henry
Demarest Lloyd, who was the *Tribune's* labor editor, reported on the
strike in vivid detail. It is necessary to rely on Lloyd's reporting since
most other midwestern newspapers virtually ignored the strike. Even
the *United Mine Workers Journal* did not cover the strike as well as did
the *Chicago Tribune*. Quoted in *Chicago Tribune*, May 30, 1894.

5. Ibid., May 24, 1894.

6. Ibid., May 27, 1894.

7. Ibid., May 26, 1894.

8. Ibid., May 28, 1894.

9. Ibid., May 29, 1894.

10. Ibid., June 9, 1894.

11. Ibid., June 10, 1894.

12. West Virginia operators, who during the 1890s produced coal
largely for a local market, saw that the strike presented them with a
good opportunity to penetrate the midwestern coal market. They kept
their employees on the job by offering them substantial wage increases.
Ibid., May 27, 1894.

13. Ibid., June 2, 4, 1894.

14. Ibid., June 11, 1894.

15. Ibid., June 12, 1894.

16. Ibid., June 18, 1894; *United Mine Workers Journal*, June 17, 1894, p. 1 (hereafter as *UMWJ*).

17. *UMWJ*, October 8, 1891, p. 2.

18. Ibid., October 22, 1891, p. 2.

19. Ibid., June 8, 1893, p. 3.

20. Ibid., October 8, 1893, p. 2.

21. Ibid., October 19, 1891, p. 3.

22. National Archives, "Manuscript Census," 1880 and 1900 (hereafter cited as "Manuscript Census").

23. For the 1892 election returns, see *Chicago Daily News Almanac, 1893* (Chicago: Daily News Press, 1894), pp. 245-67; Secretary of State, *Smull's Legislative Handbook, 1892* (Harrisburg: State Printers, 1893), pp. 443-584; Secretary of State, *Ohio Statistics, 1892* (Columbus: State Printers, 1893), pp. 356-409.

24. John Laslett, *Labor and the Left* (New York: Basic Books, 1970), p. 201.

25. *UMWJ*, March 1, 1894, p. 2.

26. Ibid., March 27, 1894, p. 2.

27. U.S. Industrial Commission, *Report of the Industrial Commission on the Relations between Labor and Capital* (Washington, D.C.: Government Printing Office, 1899), 15:394.

28. Statistics compiled by the author from *Chicago Daily News Almanac, 1895* (Chicago: Daily News Printers, 1895), pp. 243-66; Secretary of State, *Smull's Legislative Handbook, 1894* (Harrisburg: State Printers, 1895), pp. 441-552; Secretary of State, *Ohio Statistics, 1894* (Columbus: State Printers, 1894), pp. 248-406.

29. Coal towns were identified in a report that appeared as part of the 1880 census: U.S. Department of the Interior, Census Office, *Report on the Mining Industries of the United States* (Washington, D.C.: Government Printing Office, 1886). For towns that began producing coal after 1880, I went to *Proceedings of the Twentieth Annual Convention of the United Mine Workers of America, 1910* (Indianapolis: Hollenbeck, 1911), pp. 78-124. Here, one finds the location of each of the UMW's local unions. Larger cities and towns like Carbondale, Illinois, and Cambridge, Ohio, which had more noncoal miners than coal miners living in them were not classified as coal towns for the purpose of this study.

30. I arrived at the figure of 201,000 adult males by taking the total population of 724,810 (U.S. Department of Commerce, Bureau of the Census, "Population of Minor Civil Divisions, 1900," *Census of Popula-*

tion (Washington, D.C.: Government Printing Office, 1903], 3:362-98, 4:377-89) and dividing by 3.5, the average family size. This number was determined from statistics in U.S. Immigration Commission, *Reports of the Immigration Commission* (Washington D.C.: Government Printing Office, 1911), 1:21-121. The Immigration Commission determined that the coal miner families averaged 4.7 persons. However, since one-third of the coal miners were unmarried, there were on the average 3.5 people living in the average coal miner household. In 1894, while only 47 percent of the electorate in Ohio, Illinois, and Pennsylvania went to the polls, 145,859 of the coal towns' 201,000 adult male citizens, representing more than 70 percent of the electorate, voted. Usually coal town residents voted in about the same numbers as other citizens.

31. Secretary of State, *Ohio Statistics, 1894*, pp. 267-408.

32. For an excellent analysis of midwestern politics *see* Richard Jensen, *The Winning of the Midwest* (Chicago: University Press, 1971).

33. Secretary of State, *Ohio Statistics, 1896* (Columbus: State Printers, 1896), pp. 266-477; Secretary of State, *Smull's Legislative Handbook, 1897* (Harrisburg: State Printers, 1898), pp. 473-501.

34. Appendix E.

35. Quoted in Jensen, *Winning of the Midwest*, p. 245.

36. Quoted in *Indiana Union*, July 10, 1897.

37. Quoted in *Chicago Tribune*, August 15, 1897.

38. Quoted in *Indiana Union,* July 10, 1897.

39. Quoted in *Chicago Tribune*, August 15, 1897.

40. Ibid., July 15, 1897.

41. Ibid., July 16, 1897.

42. Ibid., July 16, 1897; *Indiana Union*, July 22, 1897.

43. Quoted in *Chicago Tribune*, August 2, 1897.

44. Ibid., August 27, 1897.

45. Ibid., July 14, 23, 1897.

46. Appendices L and M.

47. *Social Democrat* (Chicago), May 19, 1898.

48. John Mitchell to M. D. Ratchford, August 25, 1898, John Mitchell Collection, Catholic University.

49. Korson, *Coal Dust on the Fiddle*, p. 378; *UMWJ*, October 16, 1898, p. 2.

50. Arthur Suffern, *Conciliation and Arbitration in the Coal Industry of America* (Boston: Houghton Mifflin, 1915), p. 47.

51. *Galesburg* (Illinois) *Labor News*, April 15, July 5, 1899; clipping from *Chicago Chronicle*, in Eugene Debs's scrapbook, New York University; Paul Angle, *Bloody Williamson* (New York: Alfred A. Knopf, 1952), pp. 102-3.

52. *UMWJ*, July 6, 1899, p. 2; *Galesburg Labor News*, July 12, 1899.

53. *Social Democratic Herald* (Milwaukee), October 22, 1898.

54. Ibid., October 4, 1899.

55. Ibid., October 20, November 6, 1900.

56. *Peoria* (Illinois) *Labor Gazette*, December 7, 1900.

57. *UMWJ*, March 10, August 24, 1889.

58. Ibid., April 19, 1900, p. 2.

59. T. D. Nicolls to John Mitchell, June 9, 1900, John Mitchell Collection.

60. Ibid., June 11, 1900, John Mitchell Collection.

61. *UMWJ*, August 23, 1900, p. 1; Robert Cornell, *The Anthracite Coal Strike of 1902* (Washington, D.C.: Catholic University Press, 1957), p. 45.

62. Pennsylvania Bureau of the Mines, *Annual Report, 1900* (Harrisburg: State Printers, 1901), p. xliv; Cornell, *Anthracite Coal Strike of 1902*, p. 47.

63. *Scranton Tribune*, September 18, 1900. Since most newspapers had a tendency to sensationalize strike coverage, one has to be very careful when using newspapers to reconstruct what happened during industrial disputes. The *Scranton Tribune* and the Wilkes-Barre Times were so anti-labor as to be virtually useless. The *Scranton Tribune*, on the other hand, edited by progressive Democrats, appears to have been fairminded. Its detailed coverage of the anthracite coal strikes of 1900 and 1902 is quite valuable.

64. *New York Herald*, September 23, 1900, quoted in Victor Greene, *The Slavic Community on Strike* (Notre Dame: Notre Dame University Press, 1968), p. 167.

65. Quoted in the *Scranton Times*, September 22, 1900.

66. Ibid., September 23, 1900.

67. Ibid., October 13, 1900.

68. Ibid., October 15, 1900.

69. Ibid., October 2, 1900.

70. Appendix N; "Manuscript Census."

71. Appendix N; "Manuscript Census"; Wayne G. Broehl, Jr., *The Molly Maguires* (Cambridge: Harvard University Press, 1964); Robert Bruce, *1877: Year of Violence* (Indianapolis: Bobbs-Merrill, 1959).

72. Mark Hanna to John Mitchell, October 4, 1900, John Mitchell Collection; Mark Hanna in the *UMWJ*, May 8, 1902, p. 3.

73. "Proceedings of the Anthracite Coal Strike Commission," p. 1176, Michael Koiskik Collection, Pennsylvania State University (hereafter cited at "ACSC").

74. *Proceedings of the Twelfth Annual Convention of the United Mine Workers of America, 1901* (Indianapolis: Hollenbeck, 1902), pp. 8-9.

75. "ASCS," p. 6950. It is dangerous to rely on the analyses of colliery superintendents, but the foremen who testified before the Anthracite Coal Strike Commission were subjected to Clarence Darrow's skillful cross-examination.

76. On Weyl *see* Charles Forcey, *The Crossroads of Liberalism* (New York: Oxford University Press, 1961), pp. 52-88.

77. Walter Weyl, "Mine Discipline and Unionism," *Outlook* 26 (July 1902): 732.

78. "ACSC," p. 389; *UMWJ*, July 10, 1901, p. 1.

79. Fred Dilcher to John Mitchell, August 24, 1901, John Mitchell Collection.

80. John Mitchell to Ralph Easley, March 13, 1902, National Civic Federation Papers, New York Public Library; John Mitchell to E. B. Thomas, Erie Railroad, October 31, 1901, John Mitchell Collection.

81. "Minutes of the Tri-district Convention held on May 4-7, 1902," Michael Koiskik Collection.

82. John Mitchell to Mark Hanna, May 22, 1902, John Mitchell Collection.

83. "ACSC," p. 850.

84. *Scranton Times*, July 2, 1902; "ACSC," pp. 3984-4362.

85. Mary Harris Jones, *The Autobiography of Mother Jones* (Chicago: Charles Kerric, 1924), p. 91.

86. Testimony of F. P. Bellar before the "ACSC," pp. 4078-169.

87. Ibid., p. 432.

88. Fred Dilcher to John Mitchell, August 21, 1902, John Mitchell Collection.

89. George Hartlein to John Mitchell, August 16, 1902, John Mitchell Collection.

90. Greene, *Slavic Community on Strike*, p. 190.

91. "ACSC," pp. 4309-88.

92. *Scranton Times*, July 31, 1902.

93. Quoted in "ACSC," p. 4627.

94. Ibid., p. 4616.

95. *Scranton Times*, August 4, 5, 1902; "ACSC," pp. 3607-4900.

96. "ACSC," p. 4373.

97. Ralph Easley to George Perkins, August 3, 1902, the National Civic Federation Papers.

98. Marcus Alonzo Hanna, "Industrial Conciliation and Arbitration," *Annals of the American Academy of Political and Social Science* 40 (December 1902): 28-29.

99. Quoted in Philip Foner, *A History of the Labor Movement: The*

Policies and the Practices of the American Federation of Labor (New York: International, 1962), p. 98.

100. Ralph Easley to George Perkins, August 27, 1902, National Civic Federation Papers.

101. Anthracite Coal Strike Commisson, *Report to the President on the Anthracite Coal Strike* (Washington, D.C.: Government Printing Office, 1903).

102. A Wilkes-Barre miner to John Mitchell, September 23, 1902, John Mitchell Collection.

103. John Mitchell to Mark Hanna, September 3, 1902, John Mitchell Collection.

104. Strike relief figure taken from a June 23, 1903, memorandum, Socialist Party Collection, Duke University.

105. Leaflet distributed by the Socialist party quoted in *New York Worker*, June 8, 1902.

106. W. E. Clark to A. W. Lentz, June 10, 1903, describes the standard Socialist speech, Socialist Party Collection.

107. Socialist leaflet quoted in *New York Worker*, June 8, 1902.

108. Socialist leaflet quoted in ibid., May 25, 1902.

109. *Chicago Socialist*, June 9, September 13, 1902; Ira Kipnis, *The American Socialist Movement* (New York: Columbia University Press, 1952), p. 134.

110. William Mailley, "The Anthracite Coal Strike," *International Socialist Review* (August 1902): 83.

111. *Chicago Socialist*, October 4, 1902; *Cleveland Citizen*, June 28, 1902.

112. Quoted in *New York Worker*, October 14, 1902.

113. Normally about 50 percent of the citizens living in anthracite coal towns voted. In November 1902, 41,348 of a possible 54,000 voters went to the polls. U.S. Immigration Commission, *Report of the Immigration Commission* (Washington, D.C.: Government Printing Office, 1911), 16:588-627. According to the Immigration Commission, 75 percent of the coal miners were foreign born who did not qualify for the franchise. Thus out of the approximately 993,000 people livng in these 255 coal towns only 248,000 were citizens. Since coal miner families averaged 6.29 persons, and one-third of the anthracite miners were unmarried, average household size was 4.6, which means there were approximately 54,000 adult male citizens living in the 255 anthracite coal towns. Population statistics were calculated from U.S. Bureau of the Census, "Population of Minor Civil Divisions, 1900" (Washington, D.C.: Government Printing Office, 1903), 4:377-88.

114. On the Anti-Machine party, see *Scranton Times*, October 26, 1902.

115. "Manuscript Census."

116. Secretary of State, *Smull's Legislative Handbook, 1902* (Harrisburg: State Printers, 1903), pp. 617-39. Large cities with heterogeneous populations like Wilkes-Barre and Scranton were not included in this list of coal towns.

117. Communities where violence was particularly savage were identified in the report of Brigadier General Thomas Stewart, dated September 27, 1902, "ACSC," p. 4622.

Peace and the Failure of Socialism

CHAPTER 4

The bitter coal strikes of the late nineteenth and early twentieth centuries had given the budding American Socialist movement a chance to achieve considerable power within the United Mine Workers. Although the Socialists never took over the organization's national administration, they did succeed in developing considerable influence at the state and local levels. Yet success within the union hierarchy did not guarantee success in converting rank-and-file miners to socialism. The union's very ability to force the operators to increase wages and improve working conditions made it difficult for radicals to convince miners that real progress required abolishing so seemingly adaptable a capitalist system.

As the largest industrial union in the United States, the UMW was a prime target for Socialist organizers. Eugene Debs, perhaps the most effective among such men, was convinced that workers would vote Socialist once organized into militantly led industrial unions and set his sights on the UMW as early as 1897. His efforts during the coal strike of that year were wholehearted. When UMW president M. D. Ratchford asked for help, Debs cancelled a planned speaking tour of the Midwest in order to agitate among nonstriking miners in West Virginia. Although Debs failed to convert any large number of West Virginians to either socialism or unionism, he won much gratitude from the union. "No name is more revered, nor no voice accorded a more respectful and attentive hearing than that of Eugene Debs," asserted the *United Mine Workers Journal* in 1898.[1] During the next two decades, miners continued to listen attentively to Debs. The Socialist party's perennial presidential candidate often spoke before UMW conventions, while union officials often accompanied him during campaigns in the coalfields.[2]

Debs was particularly well received in the Illinois coal county, the center of UMW socialist power. By 1910, the state's District 12, whose membership of 80,000 made up about one-quarter of the union's total, was largely under the control of the Socialists. John Walker, the president of the district, had been converted to socialism at an early age. Upon arriving in the United States from Scotland in 1882 at the age of ten, Walker at once had been forced to go to work in the collieries to help support his family. A year later when his father, an active organizer for the Knights of Labor, was blacklisted, the Walker family had little choice but to move west, settling in Oklahoma. When he returned to Illinois in 1894, John, now twenty-two years old and a pick miner whose skills were already becoming obsolete, went to work recruiting members for the fledgling UMW. His resolute work in the national coal strike of that year won Walker the presidency of his local union. In 1902, he was elected president of the Danville subdistrict, and two years later, soon after joining the Socialist party, he was chosen to sit on District 12's executive board. He held this position until 1906, when, at the age of thirty-four, he was elected to serve as president of the Illinois district.[3]

Walker was a moderate Socialist. He could passionately denounce the injustices of the capitalist system while, at the same time, pleading with the miners to have faith in John Mitchell, who was happy enough to work with the conservative NCF to increase wages and improve working conditions. Although Walker's politics were sincerely Socialist, he never publicly criticized the conservative politics of the UMW's president.[4]

Other Illinois Socialists rarely went much beyond Walker's moderation. Although Duncan McDonald, District 12's secretary-treasurer from 1910 until 1917, was more radical than Walker in his politics, he too remained friendly with Mitchell.

Adolph Germer, secretary-treasurer of the Bellville subdistrict, usually stood alone when he criticized John Mitchell's conservatism. Germer, immigrating to the United States from Germany in 1888, had gone to work in the collieries at age ten. He became the conscience of the Illinois Socialists, often berating Walker and McDonald for betraying the Socialist faith. Extremely active as a party member, Germer wrote frequently for the Socialist press. In 1913, shortly after being narrowly defeated in a race for district vice-president, he was elected to the Socialist party's National Executive Committee. There he aligned himself with Victor Berger and the revisionists, lending his power to the campaign to recall Bill Haywood from the party's National Executive Committee.[5]

Illinois was not the only Socialist-led district in the UMW. The Socialist Francis Freehan was president of the 50,000-member Pittsburgh district from 1907 until 1914, and comrade W. D. Van Horn was president of the 20,000-member Indiana district for much of the prewar period.[6] Together these Socialist-led districts—Illinois, Indiana, and Pittsburgh—had about 150,000 members, almost half of the union's total. In 1909, a year after John Mitchell's retirement from the presidency, the Socialists nearly elected John Walker to head the UMW. Walker lost by less than 16,000 votes to Tom Lewis, the union's longtime vice-president, who had succeeded Mitchell in 1908. Walker, ironicaly, might well have triumphed if he had been able to carry his own home district convincingly. There, however, he had always faced the spirited opposition of Frank Farrington, a conservative but influential representative on the executive board. Walker carried the Indiana district by a six-to-one margin and the Pittsburgh district by more than two to one, but in Illinois Farrington's opposition kept his margin to a narrow 25,337 1/2 to 22,482 1/2. That left him with too few votes to overcome an overwhelming lead Lewis had won in the anthracite region.[7]

Despite Walker's defeat, the radicals managed to get a so-called Socialist resolution approved by the convention. John Mitchell had always successfully opposed such a resoluton while he was president, but with him in retirement, the UMW went on record as supporting the "necessity of public ownership and

democratic operation of the means of production and
exchange . . . so that every man and woman willing to
work . . . [could have] free access to the means of life and get the
full social value of his product."[8]

In 1911, two years after the passage of the resolution, the
UMW finally came to grips with John Mitchell's membership in
the National Civic Federation. The issue was crystallized when
Thomas Kennedy, the twenty-four-year-old president of an anthracite local union, introduced the following resolution at the
annual UMW convention:

The National Civic Federation which is chiefly composed and wholly
financed by the Belmonts, Carnegies, Morgans, and other bitter enemies
of organized labor, is in existence only for the sole purpose of regarding
the progress of the labor movement. . . .

In order to accomplish that end it became necessary for that institution to crush the ever growing militant spirit and advanced thought that
permeates the ranks of the labor movement. . . . The said National Civic
Federation, through its paid emissaries of all varieties, is industriously
disseminating the infamous doctrine of "identity of Interests" and
Brotherhood of Labor and Capital, a doctrine based absolutely on
economic falsehood and once firmly implanted in the minds of the
organized wage earner will surely bring about the result desired by the
employers of labor. . . .

Resolved, that each and every member of the UMW of A. is hereby
prohibited, under penalty of expulsion from affiliating with, or render-
ing aid to, financial or otherwise, the aforesaid labor-hating and design-
ing National Civic Federation.[9]

As soon as this resolution was introduced, Socialists John
Walker and Adolph Germer rose to Mitchell's defense. Although
Walker admitted that the NCF's avowed aim was to "chloroform
the labor movement politically and economically," he stead-
fastly maintained that "any man who tried to chloroform John
Mitchell and have him use his services for the detriment of labor
[had] . . . a job to accomplish."[10] Walker and Germer introduced
a substitute resolution that sought to condemn the NCF without requiring John Mitchell's expulsion from the union. Walker
claimed that Mitchell would never have joined the federa-

tion had the leader not been convinced that he could "accomplish some good for the labor movement," but this argument had little effect on the convention, and the resolution was defeated." The Kennedy measure carried. Mitchell was faced with the choice of either resigning from the UMW or the NCF. After much deliberation, he left the NCF to remain with the UMW.

The support of Mitchell by Walker, Germer, and McDonald indicated that these men appreciated the former president's position. Like their former leaders, these Socialist union officials were convinced that the miners had to reach an accommodation with the operators. Although they believed that the class struggle would continue as long as capitalism existed, they did not anticipate an early breakdown of the American political economy. For them, trade unionism was the only practical way for the working class to improve its conditions. So despite their politics, they echoed John Mitchell in maintaining that a union that expected capitalists to bargain had to "do its best to carry out its contracts."[12]

As followers of revisionist Socialists like Germany's Eduard Bernstein and America's Victor Berger, the UMW Socialists believed that real power for their party required control of the AFL. Influence within the labor movement would allow them, they thought, to persuade the working class to vote for socialism. They recognized how slow and laborious this process of "boring from within" would be but believed that in the long run such tactics would prove to be more practical than the more militant ones long advocated by the IWW's William Haywood. Walker, Germer, and McDonald saw no hope that Haywood's program of constant and restless class conflict would radicalize the working class. Reliance on such tactics, they maintained, would alienate the majority of Americans.

The UMW Socialists thus were left, as trade unionists, with bargaining for increased wages and improved working conditions. After the reestablishment of the Joint Conference in 1898, Walker, McDonald, and Germer met each January with miners and operators representing every district in the Central Competitive Field to negotiate a contract. A few years' experience under this system convinced them, as Duncan McDonald remarked, that "while it [was] . . . not ideal and [would] . . . not entirely solve the labor problem," it was "a decided improvement over the old system of gorilla [*sic*] warfare."[14] No one could seriously dispute this. Between 1898 and 1903, the Joint Conference helped raise the wages of the soft-coal miners from $270 to $522 a year. The UMW's gains in the 1902 anthracite strike had brought hard-coal miners similar prosperity. Within six years, their annual wages rose from $261 to $572. Adjusted for inflation of the time, such increases meant that real wages went up by about 50 percent.[15]

Coal mine operators were able to accept the higher wages of collective bargaining in view of other advantages. The Joint Conference agreement clearly stated that the UMW would play a crucial role in maintaining the stable conditions in the industry by "affording all possible protection to the trade . . . against any unfair competition resulting from a failure to maintain scale rates."[16] This clause meant that the union would use its power to make sure that both the operators and the miners would adhere to an equalized wage scale so that no mine owner would be placed at competitive disadvantage. As John Mitchell told the U.S. Industrial Commission, "[It is] a fundamental principle of our interstate movement that the scale of prices is based not upon the earning capacity of the miners alone, but principally upon the opportunity of each district to produce coal at a price which shall enable it to be sold in fair competition with every other district.[17]

Collective bargaining had other advantages from the coal operators' point of view. It guaranteed a disciplined work force and labor peace. "With honest and conservative men at the head of our labor organizations," said Francis Robbins, president of the Pittsburgh Coal and Coke Company, "the liability of having trouble is decreased and it is a safer method of settling wage questions than by dealing with the rank and file employee."[18]

Herman Justi, secretary of the Illinois Coal Operators Association, was pleased, especially by the system's effect on radicals. "I believe in the system of Trade Agreements," he declared in 1905:

I believe it will soon be the universal system. I favor it because it tends to broaden and enlighten those who participate in it. I favor it because I believe it will eliminate from the ranks of employers and employees the men who are responsible for what is known as cut-throat competition, a policy that is responsible for low wages and further it will ultimately drive from positions of trust and honor in the labor organizations a class of ruffians who are its greatest disgrace, a class of men half fools and half rogues.[19]

Justi, like the other coal mine operators, had concluded after the bitter strikes of the 1890s that trade unionists could be very useful in controlling rank-and-file miners. The operators cared little whether the new disciplinarians voted Republican, Democratic, or even Socialist, so long as contract terms were guaranteed. Justi hoped that the Joint Conference would lead miners to conclude that they and their bosses had "reciprocal, if not common interests," with industrial peace the result. The Joint Conference system, he declared lyrically, brought together "kindred souls of different walks of life, who otherwise might have been drawn further and further apart, increasing the bitterness felt by one for the other, of one class for the other." Without such collective bargaining, he believed, "long and bitter conflict would have been inevitable." Instead, now there was a good chance that "unreasoning radicals [would become] . . . wise and helpful conservatives."[20]

Even the anthracite operators, who had fought the UMW at every turn, had concluded by the second decade of the twentieth century that collective bargaining had benefits. Although they did not formally recognize the UMW until 1916, many anthracite operators, like their bituminous counterparts, praised the union for having "developed discipline in the men." Charles B. Doughtery of the Susquehanna Coal Company was convinced that the UMW contracts "had resulted in educating the men in the rights of their employer to a noticeable degree." R. J. Richards of the Philadelphia and Reading Railroad also favored "the trade agreement because it brought about better relations between employer and employee."[21]

The coal mine operators were speaking from solid self-interest. Wanting peace at almost any price, the officials of the UMW had become quite cautious. This continued to be true even of Socialists within the union's leadership, who presumably were conscious of the price they were paying. In 1910, for example, John Walker negotiated an agreement with the Illinois operators that gave foremen the right to dismiss any man who was absent from work without a valid medical excuse. Henry Kassenbein, a black delegate to District 12's annual convention, objected to the clause "as making all men, like my people used to be, slaves." For Walker, however, a contract was a contract, and no protest would keep the union from showing "that it respected a contract which it [had] . . . negotiated.[22]

Behavior such as this enraged some orthodox Marxists; Theodore Debs, Eugene's brother, was one. He accused Walker in 1912 of "floating Socialist and radical colors to enlist confidence and gain support so he might serve reactionary ends."[23] Not being an active trade unionist himself (he had long served labor's cause chiefly as his brother's aide), Theodore Debs could not appreciate the dilemma that Walker, McDonald, and Germer faced. As union leaders, they had to bargain for wages as high as possible. Effective bargaining—that is, bargaining in good faith—required guaranteeing that the miners would not walk off their jobs in violation of contracts. Their disciplinarian role, they could and did argue, was inevitable.

Yet the UMW Socialists must have realized that the Joint Conference was blunting the class struggle many Marxists counted on to radicalize the working class. Once wages began to rise, rank-and-file miners began to acquire a stake in the existing prosperity. "Conditions have improved in every respect since the adoption of the trade agreement," declared W. N. Eaton, a veteran of twenty-two years in the Illinois coalfields.[24] Joe Petrough, a Lithuanian immigrant who lived and worked near Springfield, Illinois, agreed: "I can read the agreement and it tells the company what it must do. If everyone would do as the agreement says it would be alright." Another immigrant coal miner, who worked in the Pittsburgh district, concurred with this judgment. "The union treats me alright," he testified before a government commission, "and it adjusts my grievances if it can. The agreement is alright. If the officers of the union sign the agreement, it must be alright. This agreement has helped me because my grievance was looked after by the union."[25]

Grievance procedures were an integral part of the trade agreement. In the Central Competitive Field grievance machinery was set up almost immediately after the 1897 strike was settled. When miners believed that they were being treated unfairly, they complained to their pit committee, a group of men elected by members of a local union to represent them in dealings with the foremen. Often the chairman of the pit committee would belittle the miners' grievances, telling them to obey the foremen and "if at the end of the day, you think you haven't made enough money because of your instructions, and if you can't settle it with him [the foreman], then bring your complaint to us."[26] Management often asked the chairman of the pit committee to help make sure that the men obeyed the provisions of their contracts. Foremen, still hard pressed to supervise all the men who worked under them, often relied on the pit committees to discipline the miners. Gone were the days of the nineteenth-century coal miners who often worked with little supervision. Gone too were their successors who had been driven unmercifully by foremen and supervisors. The new miners now had pit committees and foremen who enforced contract provisions within a standard eight-hour day.[27]

When pit committees and foremen were not able to resolve differences, mine superintendents and a union subdistrict president tried to find a solution. On difficult problems, a representative of the union's executive board would meet with a commissioner of the operator's association. Further disagreement could then bring a meeting of the union's executive board with the entire operator's association. Customarily such a meeting would not be adjourned until the problem was resolved. Except perhaps in the last hours of such rare marathon meetings, grievances were settled in a rational, unemotional atmosphere. Conflict was avoided since both parties were forbidden to take the law into their own hands. The miner kept working until the peace seekers solved his problem. Aggrieved miners who walked off their jobs in violation of contracts were subject to fine. A penalty clause in most contracts mandated a three-dollar fine for each day off the job without a valid medical excuse. Management was fined one dollar a day for each man illegally locked out, showing that, in this case, one side was clearly more equal than the other.[28]

Union officials did everything possible to keep their men on the job. Virtual indictments were handed down against wildcat strikers, followed by trial according to union rules. John Walker presided over such a proceeding at LaSalle, Illinois, on April 5, 1906. The men there had struck because they were being forced to dig coal in knee-deep water. Walker offered no sympathy to the miners; instead he spoke to them as if they were naughty children:

There are moments in life where a man has to perform a very unpleasant duty. I came here with the hope that you would justify yourself for having shut down the mine last month. Now my hope has been deceived.

Walker read the penalty clause in the union contract and continued:

You have violated your contract. This . . . contract is not perfect. . . . But it is uniformly much better than what we had before. To obtain this contract many miners have courageously fought, millions of dollars have been spent by the union, many men and women have not hesitated to undergo the bitterest hardships to conquer this contract, and you now believe that your fellow miners will allow you to break this contract simply because it pleases you do do so.[29]

Performances like this by trusted union officials who were also known to be Socialists probably did much to tame the spirit of the miners. The men were urged time and time again to exercise self-discipline and soon began to internalize this message. Even miners who resented Walker's patronizing tone had to admit that union officials spoke much truth. One LaSalle miner conceded:

You would not even recognize those Italians if you had come to this place ten years ago, before we made our agreements with the company. In that time I tell you my son, life was unbearable for us. We were working such long hours that we were too tired on Sunday to get off our beds, and yet we earned so little that women and children had to go around and beg from the bosses. Now everything has changed; we have doubled our wages, and we work only eight hours a day. All of the comfort you see here is only ten years old; ten years ago you would not have found a stove in an Italian's home.[30]

With miners feeling this way, wildcat strikes became quite rare. "Relations between foreman and employee are much more harmonious," one miner declared. "The trade agreement, once entered into," observed an Ohio local leader, "is surprisingly observed until its expiration, thus preventing strikes or variation of wages and giving stability to the industry." He went on to recall how in the past "four or five strikes [had] . . . to be called when the prices were advancing in an effort to obtain better wages, and four or five more the following year in an effort to prevent a reduction in wages." James Kelley, president of an Illinois subdistrict, believed that conditions had "become far more favorable for the workers [because] . . . grievances [were] . . . usually settled without a strike."[31]

The Slavic and Italian miners, who by 1910 numbered 60 percent in the bituminous fields and 80 percent in the anthracite, presented a special problem for the UMW.[32] "Most of the grievances complained of grew out of attempts on the part of foremen to impose on immigrant laborers," an Italian organizer, John Barafaldi, observed. "It is difficult sometimes to control them, though they can be reasoned with to some extent."[33] Many of these men, especially in the bituminous coal fields, had arrived after the great strikes and had little understanding of what the trade agreement had done for (and to) the other miners. Moreover, largely the products of east European peasant societies, they were new to industrial discipline, especially one based on paper contracts. Disciplining these men presented many difficulties. Time and again, union leaders would be heard begging the newcomers "not to compromise their great union, which always stood reeady to do everything possible for them." When immigrant miners screamed "strike, strike," local union leaders answered:

Don't give them a chance to call you uncivilized by breaking the agreement and by striking. You have an opportunity to get redress through the Board of Conciliaton. . . . Only barbarians are impatient. Civilized men wait for legal redress of grievances.[34]

For the new Americans also, the message soon became internalized. Foremen, of course, kept discriminating against Slavs and Italians by assigning them the worst places to dig coal. The UMW, nevertheless, eventually convinced the immigrants not to strike every time they had a grievance. By the middle of the second decade of the twentieth century, Duncan McDonald could assert proudly that the "union did much to dampen the immigrants' tendency to suspend work wherever a grievance . . . [arose]."[35] McDonald was celebrating the success of a process that had begun long before under John Mitchell's leadership. "You can just bet if John Mitchell says strike, den we's all will strike," one new immigrant said back in 1903, "and if he don't den we know he doesn't want us to and den we don't. John Mitchell, he knows what is best for us to do. Don't he?"[36]

The miner's closing query was rhetorical in 1903 and ever more so thereafter. The UMW leadership eventually managed to control the miners and enforce trade agreements strictly. Occasional breakdowns in the Joint Conference system did occur, marked by strikes every two years between 1906 and 1915, but neither the miners nor the operators sought any basic changes in the system.[37]

So class conflict was blunted in the unionized coalfields. The UMW Socialists continued trying to persuade the miners to vote for socialism. The pages of the *United Mine Workers Journal* continued to be used to campaign for Socialist candidates. Every few weeks, the *Journal* would reprint the party's platform, along with a commentary by John Walker or Adolph Germer. The accompanying material took on the air of a litany:

Against the two capitalist parties stands the Socialist party with its working class platform, and working class considerations. . . . The class demarcation will not be eliminated by a change from Republican to Democratic party. . . . This class demarcation springs from the private ownership of the means of production.[38]

Evidently no one noticed such pronouncements enough to object to them. Certainly they had little, if any, reflection in the election returns. Men who after violent strikes had voted for Populist or Socialist candidates returned to traditional Democratic or Republican allegiances soon after peace was restored. Perhaps the IWW had been correct in arguing that strikes, particularly bitter ones, were the only way to raise "the standard of consciousness and aggressiveness of the working class."[39] Certainly the UMW Socialists failed dismally in trying to radicalize the miners, while simultaneously enforcing collective-bargaining agreements that increased wages and improved working conditions. Table 4.1, which analyzes presidential election returns from 751 coal towns in Ohio and Pennsylvania, shows the completeness of their failure. Again, as in previous elections, ethnic and religious divisions proved to be more important than class. Protestant coal miners tended to vote for the Republican party, while Catholics voted Democratic. The Socialists never managed to win more than 11 percent of the vote.[40]

Table 4.1
PRESIDENTIAL VOTE IN 751 COAL TOWNS, 1904-1920

Year	Republican	Democrat	Socialist	Progressive	Percent Socialist
1904	76,024	44,828	6,029		5
1908	95,075	76,716	7,649		5
1912	42,568	60,137	22,210	71,491	11
1916	82,623	72,347	8,595		5
1920	109,834	60,361	964		0.5

The large Progressive vote of 1912 might indicate widespread miner dissatisfaction with the established political parties, but the miners voted for Theodore Roosevelt in only slightly larger numbers than did the population at large.[41] Nor could the Progressive party, largely financed by George Perkins of the United States Steel Corporation and Mark Hanna's son, Frank, be considered a radical substitute for confirmed Socialists.

Theodore Roosevelt's charisma might temporarily have wooed miners away from the established political parties. These same men, nevertheless, refused to take a similar step when their own union leaders—John Walker, Adolph Germer, and Duncan McDonald—appealed for support on the Socialist line. In 1906, John Walker ran as a Socialist for Congress from a district in which between 15,000 and 20,000 coal miners lived. He received only 1,551 votes.[42] Six years later Walker tried again, but with even less success. Adolph Germer and Duncan McDonald, both of whom repeatedly ran as Socialists for the Illinois state legislature, did just as poorly politically. Their coal mining districts never gave them more than 5 percent of the vote.[43] In 1906, while all three of the Illinois Socialists were going down to resounding defeat, William B. Wilson, the UMW's secretary-treasurer, and T. D. Nicolls, president of District One in the anthracite region, were elected to Congress from Pennsylvania. They, however, ran as Democrats.

Nineteen hundred and six was one of organized labor's most active political years. In March, the American Federation of Labor drew up a Bill of Grievances that sought to rally support for its campaign against the open shop drive and the use of injunctions in labor disputes. As part of this effort, more than 30 miners ran for political office, but only those like Wilson and Nicolls, who were willing to work with the major parties, found that they had any hope for success. Wilson's election from the fifteenth congressional district in Pennsylvania's bituminous region marked the beginning of his important political career, which culminated in his becoming Secretary of Labor in Woodrow Wilson's cabinet. This gave the United Mine Workers an important voice in Washington but added to the problems of the UMW Socialists. It now became increasingly difficult to con-

vince the miners that socialism was their only avenue to political
power.

NOTES

1. *United Mine Workers Journal,* August 6, 1897, p. 2 (hereafter cited
as *UMWJ*).
2. Eugene Debs to Adolph Germer, October 8, 1901, Adolph Germer
Collection, Wisconsin State Historical Society.
3. John Laslett, *Labor and the Left* (New York: Basic Books, 1970) p.
206; *see also* the biographical material in the John Walker Collection,
University of Illinois at Urbana.
4. John Mitchell to John Walker, August 2, 1911, John Mitchell Collection, Catholic University of America.
5. Germer's Bellville subdistrict contained about one-quarter of the
Illinois district's total membership. Laslett, *Labor and the Left*, p. 206;
Lorin Lee Cary, "Adolph Germer from Labor Agitator to Labor Professional" (Ph.D. diss., University of Wisconsin, 1968), pp. 1-109.
6. For a discussion of Francis Freehan and W. D. Van Horne's
political affiliations, *see Appeal to Reason,* February 6, 1909.
7. *Proceedings of the Nineteenth Annual Convention of the United Mine
Workers of America, 1909* (Indianapolis: Hollenbeck, 1910), pp.
1064-1152 (hereafter cited as *UMW Proceedings*). See appendix J.
8. Quoted in *Appeal to Reason,* February 6, 1909.
9. *UMW Proceedings,* 1909, p. 521.
10. Ibid., p. 527.
11. Ibid., p. 540; Laslett, *Labor and the Left*, p. 215.
12. Duncan McDonald before the 1910 convention of District 12,
"Proceedings of the Annual Convention of the United Mine Workers
District 12," p. 10, microfilm copy at Cornell University (hereafter cited
as "District 12 Proceedings").
13. Adolph Germer to Kier Hardie, February 18, 1913, Germer
Collection.
14. Duncan McDonald before the 1910 convention of District 12,
"District 12 Proceedings," p. 10.
15. Rising tonnage rates did not account for the entire wage increase.
With the return to prosperity in 1898 (in 1903 in the case of the
anthracite region) unemployment became a less serious problem.
Miners who during the 1890s worked between 150 and 170 days a year
were, by 1904, employed 200 days a year. *See* appendices H and I. For a

description of the way the Joint Conference worked, *see* Lewis Bloch, *Labor Agreements in the Coal Industry* (New York: Russell Sage, 1931).

16. "The Movement of Wages Among Coal Mine Workers," *Bureau of Labor Statistics Bulletin* 51 (1904):393.

17. U.S. Industrial Commission, *Final Report* (Washington, D.C., 1900-1902) 12:698.

18. Francis Robbins to John Mitchell, March 26, 1904; *see also* Henry D. Taylor to W. D. Ryan, March 4, 1904, both in John Mitchell Collection.

19. Speech by Herman Justi at Peoria, Illinois, quoted in the *UMWJ*, September 7, 1905, p. 3. For more on Justi's views *see* U.S. Industrial Commission, *Report of the Industrial Commission on the Relations between Labor and Capital* (Washington, D.C.: Government Printing Office, 1899), 14:646-78.

20. Justi in *UMWJ*, September 7, 1905.

21. Commission on Industrial Relations, "Miners and Operators on the Joint Scale" (unpublished report deposited in the National Archives, 1915), pp. 130-42 (hereafter cited as "CIR").

22. "Proceedings of District Twelve's Reconvened 1910 Convention," p. 33 (microfilm copy at Cornell University).

23. Theodore Debs to Adolph Germer, January 23, 1912, Eugene Debs Collection, New York University.

24. "CIR," p. 34.

25. Ibid., pp. 41-43.

26. Ed Weick, "A Coal Miner's Journal," *Atlantic Monthly* (July 1924): 13-15.

27. Ibid. p. 18. In the anthracite region the grievance procedures that were established in 1903 were quite primitive. A single board of conciliation, consisting of three miners and three operators, sat in judgment on all grievances. This overburdened board always had a tremendous backlog of cases, forcing miners to wait months for a hearing. Finally in 1912, the miners and operators agreed to establish more sophisticated grievance procedures, resembling those that had been functioning in the Central Competitive Field for a decade and a half.

28. Bloch, *Labor Agreements in the Coal Industry*, p. 245.

29. Quoted in Philippe Millet, "A Trial in the Coal Mines," *Outlook* 89 (December 1908):78.

30. Ibid., p. 89.

31. "CIR," p. 34.

32. U.S. Immigration Commission, *Report of the Immigration Commissioner* (Washington, D.C.: Government Printing Office, 1909), 6:34.

33. 'CIR,'' p. 57.

34. Ibid., p. 6.

35. Ibid., p. 33.

36. Quoted in *Quincy* (Illinois) *Labor News*, May 2, 1903.

37. For statistics on time lost as a result of strikes, *see* U.S. Geological Survey, *Mineral Resources in the United States* (Washington, D.C.: Government Printing Office, 1892-1921).

33. *UMWJ*, October 17, 1912, p. 2.

39. *Industrial Worker*, December 8, 1910, quoted in Philip Foner, *The Industrial Workers of the World* (New York: International, 1965), p. 136.

40. *See* appendices L, M, and N. Unfortunately, township election returns are not available for Illinois and INdiana after 1896. The returns from Ohio and Pennsylvania show that coal town voter turnout was about 51 percent. These states' 751 bituminous coal towns had a population of 1,410,000 people, approximately 1,010,000 of whom were citizens. Since average family size was 4.7 and one-third of the coal miners were unmarried, it has been calculated that there were about 290,000 adult male citizens living in these 751 coal towns. In an average election, between 150,000 and 160,000 of them went to the polls. The population statistics were calculated from U.S. Department of Commerce, Bureau of the Census, "Population of Minor Civil Divisions," *Census of Population, 1910* (Washington, D.C.: Government Printing Office, 1914), 3:430-637; statistics on family size, number of immigrants, and percentage of unmarried coal miners are from U.S. Immigration Commission, *Reports of the Immigration Commission* (Washington, D.C.: Government Printing Office, 1911), 1:21-121.

41. In Ohio and Pennsylvania Roosevelt received 29 percent of the vote. In the coal towns of these states he received 34 percent of the vote.

42. This vote was less than 4 percent of the total in a district made up of Edgar, Clark, Kanakee, Vermillion, Cumberland, and Iroquois counties.

43. *Chicago Daily News Almanac, 1907* (Chicago: Daily News Printer, 1908), p. 478; *UMWJ*, November 1, 1906, p. 1; *Appeal to Reason*, November 19, 1910.

Steel: A Different Pattern of Accommodation

CHAPTER 5

The analysis of worker radicalism in America's steel towns after the turn of the century may seem to be a twice-told tale. There, too, as in the coal industry, labor-management conflict and violence produced radicalism; industrial peace ended it equally as quickly. But the pattern of accommodation in the steel industry was sufficiently different from that worked out in the coal industry to make analysis worthwhile.

The Amalgamated Association of Iron and Steel Workers, once among the strongest craft unions in the United States, was badly weakened during the 1890s by the campaigns of Andrew Carnegie and Henry Clay Frick against it. The union's decline contrasted vividly with the contemporaneous rise of the United Mine Workers. Even after 1901, when the National Civic Federationist, J. P. Morgan, bought out Andrew Carnegie to form the United States Steel Corporation, the steel industry's antiunion campaign continued to be waged with vigor. Although Morgan was doing his best to persuade the presidents of the anthracite railroads to deal with the powerful UMW, he had nothing but contempt for the now virtually shattered Amalgamated Association.

Morgan and his new U.S. Steel, nevertheless, were challenged almost at once by the beleaguered union. Although Homestead had driven it from basic steel, the union had managed to organize the tin and sheet plate branches of the industry. These had grown rapidly after 1890 and depended heavily on skilled manual labor. By the turn of the century, the union had contracts with about 75 percent of the nation's tin mills and nearly all of the sheet plate mills. Then the U.S. Steel Corporation, founded largely to avoid dangerous competition in these parts of the industry, took over. When the union demanded recognition from the new corporate managers, it was told that such recognition "was not a matter of discussion and could not even be considered."[1] The union struck on July 1, 1901, with disastrous results. Not only did it fail to gain recognition, but it lost its hold on fifteen mills.[2]

During this battle, J. P. Morgan and his primary aide George Perkins, chairman of the U.S. Steel's finance committee, had proven to be stubbornly (some might have even said strangely) uncompromising. These National Civic Federationists, for all their supposed belief in accommodation, had no intention of coming to terms with organized labor unless forced to do so. They had their own dialectic of class conflict. Weak workers' organizations were to be smashed; strong ones accommodated; the synthesis brought them labor on close to their own terms; such was the real meaning of their homilies as to "responsible" and "irresponsible" union leadership.

That all labor leaders were not unaware of the real intentions of Morgan and Perkins helps explain the UMW's 1911 censure of John Mitchell for his membership in the NCF. An Ohio local union president placed the true facts bluntly before the UMW convention that year:

The National Civic Federation had an opportunity to benefit organized labor if it desired to do so. . . . We know the steel trust has practically eliminated from its mills all vestiges of organized labor. Who are the men who control the steel trust? Are they not the same men who are in control of the Civic Federation.[3]

How well, or better, repression in one industry might serve the same purpose as accommodation in another was evident enough from what happened to steel labor costs. Between

1890 and 1910, the labor component of steel-making costs fell by almost 30 percent.[4] Unskilled workers, who by 1910 accounted for about 50 percent of the industry's labor force, were the most brutally squeezed. These men, on the average, earned $1.65 for a twelve-hour shift, about the same wage that their counterparts had earned in 1890, when a dollar was worth 25 percent more. Only skilled steelworkers managed to stay about even with inflation.[5] This was in sharp contrast to the situation in the far less profitable coal industry, where miners' real wages increased by about 50 percent during the decade and a half following the UMW's sucessful organizing drives.

Grinding twelve-hour shifts made labor in the steel mills intolerable, but management claimed that such long hours were unavoidable. Sunday and night work were essential, it claimed, since a blast furnace had to operate twenty-four hours a day, seven days a week, once it was ignited. Moreover, when managers allowed employees two days off a month, they insisted that it was necessary for other men to work double shifts. For example, beginning Monday night a man would work a night shift for six nights. He would then have twenty-four hours off, returning to the mill for a day shift on Monday. Then, he faced the "long turn," a twenty-four hour shift that supposedly enabled his partner to take a full day off.[6]

Such long hours took their toll. The wife of one steelworker declared that the men "were always under strain." She said that as time went on, her husband found "it impossible to rest up from night to night, from week to week."[7] A veteran steelworker gave a similar account. "Mighty few have stood what I have and can tell you what it is like," Jack Griswald told a reporter with mixed pride and despair:

I've been 20 years at the furnaces and been working 12 hours a day all the time, seven days a week. We all get to work at seven in the morning and we get through at seven at night. We work that way for two weeks and then we get the long turn. . . . The next time they get the long turn and we get 24 hours off. But it don't do us much good. I get home at 7:30 Sunday morning and go to bed as soon as I've had breakfast. I get up at noon to get a bit o' Sunday to enjoy, but I'm tired and sleepy all afternoon.[8]

Griswald continued by suggesting what an eight-hour day could mean for him and his family:

Now if we had eight hours it would be different. I'd come home after dinner, me and the missus could go to the park if we wanted to, or I could take my children to the country where there aren't any saloons. That's the danger, the children runnin' in the streets and me with no time to take them any place.[9]

Steelworkers had to pace themselves in order to get through an eighty-four-hour work week. "The twelve hour day [gave] . . . a very special character to the industry itself as well as to the men," one-time steelworker, Charles Walker, declared:

I remember noticing the difference in pace and tempo from that of a machine shop or a cotton mill. Men learned to cultivate deliberate movements with the view to the 12 hour stretch before them. When working with a pick axe or on some slag on my first night I was reproached and told "tak it easi otza time before 7:00."[10]

Thus the twelve-hour day was irrational even from management's point of view. As an earlier generation of steel magnates had recognized, men who worked twelve rather than eight hours a day did not produce 50 percent more steel. Jack Pfeifer, a veteran of forty-three years in the mills, pointed out that "a man can produce as much in eight hours as he does in twelve. At the end of eight hours, work practically stops; everybody drags himself along performing as little work as possible."[11]

Tired men were accident prone. Quick reactions to frequent emergencies became almost impossible. "Sometimes a chain breaks and a ladder tips over," a steelworker recounted. "If everything is working all smooth a man watches out and everything is alright. But you take it after they've been on duty twelve hours without sleep and running like hell and everybody's tired and it's all a different story."[12] When men worked with molten steel, one false move could result in the loss of an arm or leg. A worker near a crane when it collapsed or a blast furnace when it exploded was usually killed. The industry's accident rate was staggering. Between 1907 and 1910, 15 percent of the men were injured or killed each year.[13] Companies usually paid funeral expenses, but until 1911, when U.S. Steel introduced its first welfare plan, workers and their families received no other compensation. The streets of every steel town were lined with cripples begging.[14] Particularly vulnerable were the immigrants, most of whom came to the Pittsburgh district directly from an east European peasant society. Each year, one-quarter of them, totally lacking in factory experience, suffered serious accidents.[15]

Those Slavs and Italians—some 60 percent of the industry's labor force by 1908—who were not killed or badly injured enjoyed their good health at their mills' lowest wages. While skilled, mostly English-speaking men received wages as high as 40 cents an hour, the unskilled Slavs and Italians worked for 16.5 cents an hour.[16] Few immigrants rose to the ranks of the skilled, for unlike their counterparts in coal, they did not have a union. English-speaking foremen, who had promotion authority, would often tell the Slavs and Italians, "Good jobs are not for a Hunky; you are already earning too much for a Hunky."[17] Men discriminated against in this way were, on the average, able to earn only $12.50 a week, some $2.50 below current average family subsistence costs.[18]

Such Slavs and Italians had come to America in pursuit of a dream. They soon discovered, as one of them reported, "America is no better than in our country, whoever does well, he does well, and whoever does poorly he suffers misery as elsewhere. . . . Many people in our country think that in America everybody has much pleasure. No it is just as in our country."[19]

Living in poverty was not a new experience for the immigrants, but working in a steel mill certainly was. In eastern Europe, men and women could usually scratch out a living from the soil. Floods and droughts could bring ruin, but the tyranny of nature was quite different from that of foremen and the time clock. In the old country, men and women had worked from dawn to dusk during planting and harvest seasons, but at other times they labored at a more leisurely pace, with some time out for sport, drink, religious holidays, and national festivals. Once they reached the Pittsburgh district, such amenities ended.

As E. P. Thompson has observed, the transition to an industrial society "entailed severe restructuring of work habits—new disciplines, new incentives and a new human nature upon which these incentives could bite effectively."[20] Vague notions that the streets of the New World were paved with gold soon gave way to the realities of twelve hours a day, seven days a week. If the steelworkers wanted to get paid, they had to report to the mill on time and stay at their work places, performing their assigned tasks, until they were dismissed. One man vividly described the difficulty of adjustment: "People in our country imagine that when somebody comes to America he does nothing but make money. But in America one must do the work of three horses."[21] The experience was often traumatic. After twenty years in the Pittsburgh district, one man could still recall his first day on the job with horror:

The man put me in a section where there was terrible noises, shooting, thundering and lightning. I wanted to run away, but there was a big train in front of me. I looked up and a big vessel with firing was making its way toward me. I stood numb, afraid to move, until a man came to me and led me out of the mill.[22]

In time, most of the bewildered peasants were transformed into efficient industrial workers. In steel, the transformation came at the hands of foremen. Here, unlike in coal, no union stood by to help teach the immigrants what was expected of them, even the virtues of being punctual. To get similar results, the steel mills used the whip of the piecework system. To get paid the men had to produce.

This system, to the surprise and extreme discouragement of management, was not always effective. East European peasants often proved almost heroically resistant to industrial discipline. U.S. Steel, in fact, found it necessary to hire teachers to conduct midday classes, where immigrants were taught to read from books that stressed the importance of good work habits. One such lesson read:

> I go to the mill to start work.
> First I go to the CLOCK HOUSE.
> I take my number from the CARD RACK.
> I go to the CLOCK.
> I put my CARD in the CLOCK.
> I RING the CLOCK.
> The CLOCK shows the TIME TO START WORK.
> I see the sign on THE CLOCK HOUSE.
> It reads I MUST KNOW THE SAFETY RULES.
> I think of the LITTLE RULE BOOK.
> It was given at the EMPLOYMENT OFFICE.
> I must read the RULE BOOK.
> I want to know all the SAFETY RULES.
> I do not want to get hurt.
> I will be careful not to hurt the other men.
> I leave the clock house for my work.[23]

Despite such beguiling texts, Y.M.C.A. teachers often had difficulty inculcating the immigrants fully with the Puritan ethic. Centuries-old drinking habits often interfered with efficient mill operations. The saloon was the center of mill town social life. After a hard day's work, men often found these establishments much more attractive than their bleak and overcrowded tenements. They would come to talk with their friends or to see a burlesque show. Sometimes they would stay for days, drinking until money and then credit ran out. So common was such behavior that foremen could not dismiss every man who took an occasional day off. All that they and the steel magnates could do was enlist in the temperance crusade.[24]

While the escape of liquor dulled the immediate agony for some immigrant steelworkers, many others looked forward to a more permanent escape. Seeing their jobs as being only temporary, they hoped to be able to accumulate money so that they could return home and buy a farm. Living in boarding houses, with ten to twelve in a room, did make it possible for many to save. Once they had a few dollars, many steelworkers were both eager and able to leave the Pittsburgh district. Between 1908 and 1910, for example, forty-five returned home for each one hundred who arrived. "We came here hoping to find better conditions; we are going back home because we believe that we were better off there," a man buying a steamship ticket declared. "We could not stand the work here very much longer."[25]

Such sentiments help explain why only 20 percent of the immigrant steelworkers who were eligible for citizenship chose to become naturalized.[26] "As I am going back to the old country," said one, "it would not be right to give my allegiance there and make myself a citizen here."[27] Even men who could save little money because they had families with them dreamed of leaving. "We owned a little house in Hungary and had a farm. I have not taken out citizenship papers. I do not think I shall, though I see no chance to save enough to go back."[28]

English-speaking migrants from rural America often regretted, as much as the immigrants, the day they left the land. "I was born and raised on a farm not a hundred miles from here," the wife of one steelworker declared. "You can imagine how such living seems to me. Would I go back to the farm? I'd walk back, but we're too deep in debt to get out of the fix we are in."[29]

We don't live the way we were brought up to live [one steelworker complained] or the way we wish we could live. We buy one quart of milk a day for seven cents; that's $2.00 a month of our $58. We realize that five kids ought to have three quarts of milk a day, and it ought to be of better quality if they are to grow husky as we did in the country. But three quarts of milk at eight cents; what will that cost?

The man's wife also looked back to the farm: "It make me sick when I think of the milk we used to have when we were children on the farm. I was sent to school 'til I was 17. But I'm afraid none of my babies will ever see school when they are 17."[30]

The litany for many of the English-speaking workers also became, "If I had known better I would have stayed on the farm." But like the family-bound immigrants, they had no chance to save money to buy land and farm equipment. "Most of the men are just like I am and can't get enough money to make the break," one declared.[31]

Despite such hardships, the steelworkers did not rebel until the 1908-1909 depression brought about massive unemployment. This economic downturn reduced employment in the industry from 151,000 men in 1907 to 118,000 in 1908, and the annual wage of the average steelworker fell from $544 to $478.[32] Thus, in 1909, even though the industry was showing signs of recovery, the men at McKees Rocks, Butler, and Newcastle, Pennsylvania, struck. The strikers, like their brethren in coal many years before, soon faced strikebreakers. In steel, too, violence quickly became unavoidable, and at McKees Rocks in July 1909, it matched anything the earlier coal strikes had produced.

Before the recession, the men at the McKees Rocks Pressed Steel Car Company had been paid on the basis of their individual output. The company, however, took advantage of the recession to reorganize its operations. Under the new system, base pay for most unskilled workers was calculated on the output of the entire assembly line. This pooling system not only reduced tonnage rates but now deducted from 25 to 40 cents an hour from the wage pool to pay foremen. The workers, understandably, felt they were being forced to pay their bosses' salaries. With wages down as much as 30 percent to as low as one dollar a day, they found the new system intolerable.[33]

On July 10, fifty riveters at McKees Rocks Pressed Steel struck. Within a few days, they were joined by 6,000 fellow workers. On July 13, the men of the nearby Butler Steel Car Company also left their jobs. Although a pooling system had not yet been introduced there, the men feared a lost strike at McKees Rocks would make it their lot. Less directly threatened and more poorly organized than the workers at McKees Rocks, the Butler strikers soon were defeated.[34] This loss, however, only appeared to strengthen the resolve of the McKees Rocks men. They organized a coordinating committee known as the "Big Six" that assigned men to guard every approach to the plant against strikebreakers. Even the state police could not break through.

In the combat, the McKees Rocks workers seemed to forget ethnic differences. Slavs, Italians, and men of British or northwest European descent, who had rarely socialized with each other, met day after day to plan strike strategy. The English-speaking workers came to admire the immigrants' militancy. "The Slavs have a whole lot of guts," one observed. "We are trying to be men among men."[35]

Important differences, however, soon began to develop between the skilled native and unskilled foreign workers. Most of the skilled men, including chairman C. A. Wise who dominated the Big Six, were unaffected by the pooling system. These men, seeking to avoid violence, eagerly sought compromise. On July 31, when Wise offered management a settlement that did not propose to abolish the pooling system, a group of Slavs and Italians organized their own coordinating committee. This body came to be known as the Unknown Committee. The unskilled strikers followed their new leadership and enthusiastically remained on the picket lines. Most skilled workers reluctantly went along.[36]

At this juncture, the Industrial Workers of the World arrived. On August 15, William Trautman, IWW general organizer, came to McKees Rocks. Two days later 8,000 men and women attended an IWW rally. Three thousand joined the Wobblies, pledging that they "would never return to work unorganized and unprotected."[37] Partisans of the IWW found renewed hope for their dogma that "strikes would raise the standard of consciousness and aggressiveness of the working class."[38] Certainly it seemed as if class conflict was radicalizing the striking McKees Rocks steelworkers.

The IWW, however, behaved in much the same way as John Mitchell's UMW a decade earlier. The union leaders pleaded with the men to remain calm and nonviolent, but the IWW was no more successful than its more conservative predecessors in controlling men who felt their solidarity threatened. On August 22, when the Pressed Steel Car Company made its first serious attempt to import strikebreakers, the men took to the streets, stopping streetcars and searching for strikebreakers. Sheriff Harry Exler ordered the strikers to desist. Drawing his revolver, he screamed, "Get away or I'll kill every one of you." The strikers quickly surrounded the sheriff, shouting in turn, "Get off that [street] car! Put him off that [street] car!" Exler opened fire but proved to be an astonishingly bad shot. Soon, gun empty, he could only beg the crowd for mercy. No more merciful than he, and with much less reason to be, the strikers shot and killed the sheriff.[39]

Exler's death led to a bloody battle, during which enraged deputies pressed a house-to-house search for the sheriff's killers. After dozens of strikers were arrested, the steelworkers and their families felt they had no choice but to fight back. Moreover the police had begun to escort strikebreakers into the plant. It appeared as if peaceful picketing would not be sufficient to win. "They [the IWW] told us to be good and it would be alright," one enraged striker declared. "We have been good and look! There are strikebreakers in the works. . . . We have to fight now, we have been good too long." Another irate immigrant voiced similar intentions: "We go away from the old country to get away from being treated mean, and we come here and are treated worse," he screamed. "In my country we kill when we are treated mean, well we can kill here too."[40] Feeling this way and armed with guns and clubs, the strikers began attacking the police. Law-enforcement officials failed in their attempt to dislodge them from the area around the mill.

During the first week of September, C. A. Wise and his Big Six, alarmed by the violence, resurfaced. On September 8 they again went to the company with an offer of a settlement. Wise asked management to abolish the pooling system, restore the pre-1907 wage scale, and establish a minimum wage. With the company appearing to have agreed, the men returned to work. Soon, however, it became evident that management had no intention of going along with Wise's plan. Upon returning to work, the strikers found conditions to be identical to those that had existed before the strike. The IWW called for another walkout. The immigrants responded, but most of the skilled workers did not honor the picket lines. Led by Wise and marching under a huge American flag, they confronted the IWW pickets. As the procession approached, the picket line dissolved. The second McKees Rocks strike was broken.[41]

Meanwhile another battle was taking place at nearby Newcastle, where a strike had begun on June 20. The American Sheet and Tin Plate Company, one of the few subsidiaries of the U.S. Steel Corporation that still bargained with the Amalgamated Association, refused to renew its union contract. The Amalgamated men struck and were quickly joined by the mills' unskilled men. Newcastle was the headquarters of the western Pennsylvania branch of the IWW. The Wobblies soon plunged in. They organized well-attended mass meetings, where both worker solidarity and the IWW were celebrated. The Wobblies, however, proved no match for the state police, who quickly arrived. Militant picket lines were smashed. Strikers were beaten up, and both IWW and Amalgamated leaders were carted off to jail. By August the tin plate workers were forced to surrender.[42]

The steel magnates claimed that they ruthlessly suppressed the McKees Rocks and Newcastle strikes in order to defend American capitalism from the IWW, yet when the conservative AFL tried to organize steelworkers, they received the same treatment as the IWW.[43]

During the winter of 1910, Bethlehem, Pennsylvania, became a battleground. A strike there had broken out when management, trying to fill a large government contract, demanded paid but compulsory overtime of its employees. In response, the men organized militant picket lines, forcing Bethlehem Steel to shut down. During the first ten days of the conflict, the AFL managed to recruit 3,800 members. Yet despite the efforts of moderate union organizers, the Bethlehem strike turned out to be more violent than the IWW-led Newcastle walkout. Strikebreakers were pulled from streetcars and beaten, and the offices of Bethlehem Steel were repeatedly stoned. When the police tried to interfere, the steelworkers turned up armed in the streets. The resultant clashes were at least as bloody as those that had taken place in McKees Rocks the year before.[44] At the beginning, Charles Schwab, the president of Bethlehem Steel, had proclaimed that "under no circumstances [would he] . . . deal with the men on strike or with a body of men representing organized labor."[45] He failed to anticipate what circumstances desperate workers could create. On March 11, 1910, Schwab agreed to make overtime voluntary. The strikers went back to work feeling victorious.

Although the 1909-1910 steel strikes were violent, they failed to convince a significant number of steelworkers to vote for socialism. The Socialist party, under the control of Victor Berger and working for "class understanding through the development of mutual class respect," had not involved itself in the strikes, and it did not profit from them.[46] In November 1910, John Slayton, running for governor on the Socialist ticket, received 12 percent of the steel town vote, roughly the same percentage as Eugene Debs had received two years before.[47]

It was the Democrats, not the Socialists, who initially benefited from the 1908 depression and the 1909-1910 strikes. Between 1894 and 1906, the Republicans usually polled about 65 percent of the Pittsburgh district steel town vote, with the Democrats getting between 30 and 35 percent. This margin was reduced by 10 percent in 1908 and by another 5 percent in 1910.[48] In 1911, the Socialist party began to make its presence felt by launching a full-scale organizing campaign in the Pittsburgh district. When Eugene Debs came to towns like Newcastle, he found that the memories of the recent strike were still fresh. He received an enthusiastic response when he reminded the steelworkers that

when that greedy, heartless, soulless corporation, the United States Steel Corporation made up its mind to smash the only power of resistance that the workers had, the siamese twins of capitalism, the Democratic and Republican parties lined up together. They called on a Republican mayor and a Republican sheriff. They brought in the cossacks to club you in the streets.[49]

Speeches like this made a measurable impression on the Newcastle electorate. In November 1911, the citizens of Newcastle elected a Socialist mayor, William V. Tyler, and ten Socialist city councilmen out of a possible twenty-six.

Elsewhere in the Pittsburgh district, party organizers also met with success. By the fall of 1911, the Socialist party's Pittsburgh local had a membership of 2,000 and the McKeesport local had 1,500 members. Flourishing locals were also established at McKees Rocks, Braddock, Homestead, and Duquesne. All had semiautonomous Slavic, Magyar, and Jewish branches. In 1911, the Pittsburgh district Socialists ran an aggressive campaign. Reminding the steelworkers of the role the state had played in recent strikes, they succeeded in electing sheriffs and city councilmen in Pittsburgh, East Pittsburgh, West Brownsville, Wilmerding, and East McKeesport.[50]

Encouraged by these results, Eugene Debs continued to schedule speaking engagements in and around Pittsburgh. At Newcastle he told the steelworkers:

A party is simply an expression in political terms of the economic interests of those who are living today. You have interests separate and apart from your masters. They own the wealth and you do the work. You produce the wealth and they take it. So don't vote for the party of your masters. It is time to take political power for yourselves.[51]

Debs promised the steelworkers that the Socialists would redistribute America's wealth. He declared:

There are about 250,000 plutocrats in this country and they own 70 percent of the wealth; there are about eight million in the middle class and they own 25 percent of the wealth; there are 70 million workers and they own five percent of the wealth. They who do all the useful work; they who mine the coal; they who hammer the steel; they who feed and clothe and house the world; they but for whom every wheel would cease to revolve; they get just enough of what they produce under this system to keep them in working condition for their masters.[52]

Socialists campaigning in the Pittsburgh district were not afraid to call for the abolition of capitalism. John W. Slayton, whose governorship bid had been so warmly received in the anthracite region of eastern Pennsylvania in 1902, frequently

exhorted the steelworkers. "Before the conditions of the working class can become any better," he declared, "the oppressed
themselves will have to stir and then join a political party which
will wipe the profit system out of existence."[53]

Debs's and Slayton's speeches made sense to the steelworkers.
In the winter of 1912, when the UMW Socialists, long past their
era of strikes and militancy, were finding it very hard to convert
coal miners to their cause, steelworkers listened. "Now I'm a
Socialist; the steel mills have made me one," said one of them.
"When the workers wake up and vote to own the means of
production then, and not till then, can we get relief."[54] These
sentiments were reflected in the election returns. In 1912,
despite the spirited opposition of a putatively radical Progressive
party, Debs received 25 percent of the presidential vote in the
sixteen steel communities of western Pennsylvania. As table
5.1 shows, he ran second only to the Progressive party's Theodore
Roosevelt and ahead of William Howard Taft and Woodrow
Wilson.[55]

Table 5.1
1912 ELECTION IN SIXTEEN
PENNSYLVANIA STEEL COMMUNITIES

Town or City	Republican	Democrat	Socialist	Progressive
Allegheny County				
Braddock	226	411	150	500
Duquesne	119	264	335	444
East McKeesport	28	50	145	145
Homestead	247	317	305	621
McKeesport	922	1,114	1,381	1,952
McKees Rocks	130	223	146	500
North Braddock	140	294	311	334
Pittsburgh				
(steel wards)	4,929	5,257	5,193	5,954
East Pittsburgh	123	157	154	162
Rankin	103	89	73	186
West Homestead	34	69	74	89
Wilmerding	83	86	331	302
Lawrence County				
Newcastle	116	796	1,009	1,167

Table 5.1—*Continued*

Town or City	Republican	Democrat	Socialist	Progressive
Westmoreland County				
Monessen	262	189	174	492
Washington County				
Donora	246	157	141	348
West Brownsville	43	59	92	83
Total	7,751	9,532	10,014	12,729

The figure of 25 percent probably underestimates the extent of Socialist sentiment among steelworkers. Since only about 50 percent of the steelworkers were native-born or naturalized citizens, they accounted for only about one-third of the voting population of the towns. On the other hand, about 90 percent of the middle class qualified for the franchise.[56]

A somewhat clearer picture of steelworkers' voting behavior emerges from a study of the election returns from wards and precincts near the mills where worker families clustered. As table 5.2 shows, Eugene Debs received 40 percent of the vote in thirteen communities so situated.[57]

Table 5.2
1912 ELECTION IN THIRTEEN COMMUNITIES
ADJACENT TO STEEL MILLS

Town or Ward	Republican	Democrat	Socialist	Progressive
Duquesne Second Ward	30	119	135	170
East Pittsburgh				
Second Ward	25	74	78	71
Homestead Third Ward	42	52	111	161
McKeesport Eight Ward				
First Precinct	39	30	124	165
Second Precinct	32	53	141	89
Ninth Ward				
First Precinct	28	30	131	86
Eleventh Ward				
First Precinct	3	3	10	19
Second Precinct	33	41	114	75

Table 5.2—*Continued*

Town or Ward	Republican	Democrat	Socialist	Progressive
McKees Rocks				
Second Ward	41	60	268	99
Newcastle				
Fifth Ward	90	59	116	143
Sixth Ward	100	73	118	90
Seventh Ward	107	76	116	117
Eighth Ward	88	30	142	87
North Braddock				
First Ward	43	66	149	49
Wilmerding First Ward	39	30	186	87
Total	740	796	1,939	1,508

The 1910 census gave these Pittsburgh district communities a population about 75 percent Slav or Italian. It was the new immigrants, desperately trying to adjust preindustrial ways to an industrial society, who most probably produced the bulk of the Socialist vote in 1912. In sharp contrast, few English-speaking steelworkers appear to have voted for Eugene Debs. In Bethlehem, Steelton, and Johnstown City, cities where 75 percent of the population was English speaking, the Socialists received only about 5 percent of the vote. Bethlehem and Johnstown City had large Irish-Catholic populations, who usually voted Democratic. Protestant Steelton, on the other hand, was a Republican stronghold.[58]

The steel magnates were not oblivious to the meaning of the strikes of 1909-1910 and the 1911-1912 election returns. Some of the more powerful among them decided to follow the example set by the coal operators earlier and come to an accommodation with their employees. In the winter of 1912, E. H. Gary, chairman of the executive board of U.S. Steel, declared:

Unless capitalists, corporations, rich men, powerful men themselves take a leading part in trying to improve the conditions of humanity great dangers will come . . . and they will come quickly and the mob will bring them. Things are being said very similar to things said just before the French Revolution. I tell you the spark may yet ignite the flame and that soon.[59]

E. H. Gary, J. P. Morgan, and George Perkins, for all their seeming complacency, had long tried to moderate the antilabor policies of their subsidiary company presidents. They disapproved of subordinates who liked to brag that they had "one rule, if a workman sticks his head up, hit it."[60] Although the NCF group was determined not to permit the steelworkers to organize a union, it hoped to buy employee loyalty with "fair" wages, improved safety devices, and clean washrooms.[61] Gary, Morgan, and Perkins repeatedly, though usually unsuccessfully, ordered steel bosses to improve conditions in the mills. In 1907, U.S. Steel's finance committee, supposedly omnipotent in the great combine, had suggested phasing out the seven-day work week. This resolution was never implemented.

Perkins, chairman of the finance committee, pushed for profit sharing, his favorite plan. In 1903, he forced the recalcitrant presidents to permit the steelworkers to purchase preferred stock at a price slightly below market value. Beyond regular dividends, employee stockholders were promised a bonus if they remained with the company for five years and had shown "a proper interest in its welfare." "If profit sharing means anything . . . ," Perkins suggested hopefully, "it should mean the real cooperation between stockholders, managers and employees." Perkins, however, revealed his real motive when he declared that "there [was] . . . no such antidote for Socialism as profit sharing. . . . The more people share in the knowledge and the properties themselves, the more contented they will be."[62]

Perkins's dream could move from mere public relations to reality only if the steel companies were willing to pay for it. Certainly the workers could not. The 10 percent who were relatively well-paid, skilled men did invest in stock, but the vast majority, who earned under $600 a year, could not afford stock priced at between $80 and $90 a share, and they saw the profit-sharing plan as a total fraud. "The first stock issued in 1903 was followed by a slash in wages in 1904 that amounted to a lot more than they gave us in dividends," one veteran steelworker observed. "They take away more than they give in dividends, so the corporation is always ahead of the game."[63]

As long as subsidiary presidents set wage scales at the subsistence level, U.S. Steel's profit-sharing plan was probably more of an irritant than an antidote for socialism. The 1911-1912 election returns suggest as much.

The bankers and lawyers on the corporation's executive board were not unaware of how subsidiary presidents were undercutting their ameliorative labor policies. After the bitter 1909-1910 strikes, they began trying to clamp down. On October 19, 1911, E. H. Gary, with his usual sense of good public relations, instructed the subsidiary presidents to

make certain at all times that the men in your employ are treated as well, if not better, than other men who are working for people who deal and contract with unions. Make certain that you pay liberal wages and that your hours are as good as your wages are great . . . that so far as you have any control and influence your men are as comfortable in every respect as the men in any other place! And so far as you can, cultivate a feeling of friendship and influence your men to the conclusion that it is in their interests in every respect to remain in your employ.[64]

"Humaneness is the handmaiden of efficiency," declared William Dickson, the corporation's first vice-president. "We are now beginning to place more emphasis than formerly on the human element, which purely from an economic standpoint, and aside from any altruistic motives, must be kept in condition for efficient work, if we are to maintain our position in the world market."[65] In 1910, following Dickson's recommendations, U.S. Steel inaugurated a fairly sophisticated accident-prevention program. Believing that it could no longer afford to lose the services of thousands of valuable trained men each year, the company set up a special Bureau of Safety, Relief, Sanitation and Welfare.

The bureau immediately began inspecting all equipment in the steel mills. Safety guards were installed on cutting devices, and men in dangerous jobs were required to wear goggles and protective clothing. Steelworkers were constantly reminded that "carelessness is dangerous." Signs in seven languages were posted at all work areas telling the men that "it is your duty to report all unsafe conditions to your foremen and super-intendents."[66] On the whole, the safety campaign, though probably also aided by technological change, was extraordi-narily successful. In the seven years between 1911 and 1918, the accident rate in the steel mills was reduced by more than 60 percent.[67]

The Bureau of Safety, Relief, Sanitation and Welfare was re-sponsible for much more than accident prevention. It estab-lished pension and workman's compensation plans; tore down slums and replaced them with what were considered model homes; and built parks, swimming pools, schools, libraries, and hospitals. There is no question but that the bureau, on a budget of $75,000 a year, about 0.1 percent of the corpo-ration's annual gross expenditures, did its best to improve the quality of life in the Pittsburgh district. The corporation also intensified its English-language educational campaign. The books and lessons of the company-paid teachers continued to remind the steelworkers of the rewards American society had for the industrious.[68]

The demand for higher worker pay by the upper echelon of U.S. Steel officers turned out in time to be more than just talk. Between 1908 and 1914, a period marked by a 15 per-cent rise in consumer prices, the average wages of unskilled workers went up almost 50 percent, from $409 a year to $591 a year.[69] Management also finally began to phase out the eighty-four-hour work week. In 1910, before the annual meeting of the American Iron and Steel Institute, William Dickson declared, "It is my own deliberate judgement . . . that the present conditions which necessitates the employment of the same individual workman twelve hours a day for seven days a week are a reproach to our great industry and should not be toler-ated." The presidents of the corporation's subsidiary companies did not agree. Edgar Cook of the Warwick Iron and Steel Com-pany tried to convince the executive board that "if these men are not working . . . they have just enough of a beginnings of an education to get together and make themselves unhappy and dis-contented, but no resources to occupy themselves profitably."[70] Yet despite such opposition, Dickson's recommendation was accepted by the executive board. By 1912, most steelworkers were enjoying, as best they could after six twelve-hour days, one full day off from work each week.

With wages rising and the work week being shortened, the Socialists were thrown on the defensive. In 1913, the party managed to elect city councilmen in McKeesport and Wilmerding, but in the other steel towns in the Pittsburgh district, the Socialists went down to defeat. Even the Newcastle Socialist administration was swept out of office by a Democratic—Republican fusion ticket. While in office, the Newcastle Socialists had, in fact, been a disappointment to the steelworkers. Having failed to win a majority in the city council, Mayor William V. Tyler and his Socialist followers could not enact their program into law. They were even frustrated in efforts to appoint Socialists to head the police and health departments. On several occasions, the steelworkers had invaded council chambers, trying to persuade the aldermen to pass Socialist legislation, but the politicians remained unmoved.[71]

The Newcastle Socialists had customarily provided much of the spark for the party's election campaigns in the Pittsburgh district. With them now bogged down by the day-to-day frustration of city government, the region's Socialists found it impossible to organize an effective campaign. In November 1914, Joseph B. Allen, the party's candidate for governor, received only 13 percent of the steel town vote. This was more than double the support he attracted in the state's long-peaceful coal communities, but the Pittsburgh-district Socialists were understandably distressed by the 50 percent drop in their vote within two years. There was more distress to come. In 1916, only 5.5 percent of the voters who lived in steel towns cast ballots for socialism. In 1918, only 1 percent of them did so.[72]

Quite probably World War I and the "red scare" hastened the party's collapse. In addition, after the Socialists' 1917 St. Louis national convention adopted a strong antiwar platform, many steelworkers withdrew from the party to support Woodrow Wilson and the war effort. After the war, those who had remained in the party had to cope with the red scare the best they could. By the time it was over, only a handful of card-carrying Socialists remained in the Pittsburgh district. Yet the war and the red scare were not completely responsible for the party's collapse. The 1914 vote suggested that it had started well before America's entry into the war. Rising wages and welfare capitalism more than red baiting explain the decline in socialism in the Pittsburgh district.[73]

Yet in 1918, when steelworker radicalism had seemingly all but disappeared, William Z. Foster, a former Wobbly who had gained fame for his success in organizing the Chicago stockyards, persuaded a reluctant AFL to launch an organizing drive in steel. Foster and his National Committee for Organizing Iron and Steel Workers were quite successful at first. Wartime labor shortages had brought a return to the eighty-four-hour work week. Patriotic exhortation did little to lessen worker irritation. "No man ought to work more than eight hours," one asserted.[74] "The steelworkers are subjected to a slavery worse than the niggers before the Civil War."[75]

So Foster and his union organizers were warmly received. Company spies forced the men to keep their membership a secret, but they joined. By September 1919, 250,00 of the industry's 365,000 employees had signed up. Foster's National Committee felt strong enough to call a strike.[76] Some 275,000 workers walked out, an impressive showing, but the union had an achilles heel. The National Committee had not been able to persuade the relatively well-paid skilled men to join the strike. Like their counterparts in anthracite eighteen years before, these men, mostly all English-speaking, became strikebreakers. They blamed the Slavs and Italians for organizing the strike. "The foreigners who [were] . . . in control of the strike," they claimed were "out to run the mills themselves." Maintaining that they would not "sit down next to a Hunky or a nigger as you'd have to in a union," they crossed the picket lines. Even those skilled workers who were not overtly bigoted were reluctant to join the union. They held privileged positions in the mills that they feared to lose. "There are always men just waiting to take the jobs of the skilled worker," said one such man. "Ten men are waiting to pounce on my job right now."[77]

Facing such resistance, Foster and the National Committee

could not make the strike completely effective. On the picket lines, the tens of thousands of unskilled workers were joined by only about 50 percent of the English-speaking labor force. Some mills managed to remain open, and strikebreaking led to violence when the state militia and the U.S. Army tried to help the steel magnates keep their mills open. This time they succeeded. There were just too many skilled English-speaking steelworkers who were determined to cross the picket lines. By mid-December, only 109,000 men remained on strike. Four weeks later, the National Committee was forced to surrender as the strikers returned to work on management's terms.[78]

The 1919 steel strike, however, had led to a temporary Socialist revival. In 1920, Eugene Debs, running for president from the Atlanta penitentiary, polled 11 percent of the Pittsburgh district steel town vote.[79]

This upsurge in radicalism probably encouraged the steel magnates to continue their commitment to welfare capitalism. In 1921, the twenty-four-hour shift was permanently abolished. By 1924, the average steelworker had a fifty-four-hour work week. Moreover, real wages, which had increased by 30 percent during the war, remained at the 1919 level throughout most of the 1920s.[80] Thus the accommodation that had been worked out between 1911 and 1919 did not break down until the Great Depression. Not until then would steelworkers organize another union and force their bosses to deal with them collectively.

NOTES

1. Amalgamated Association of Iron and Steel Workers, "Proceedings of the 1901 Convention," p. 6046 (microfilm copy at Cornell University).

2. David Brody, *Steel Workers in America* (Cambridge: Harvard University Press, 1960), pp. 61-68; John A. Garraty, "The United States Steel Corporation versus Organized Labor," *Labor History* 1 (Winter 1960): 6-12.

3. United Mine Workers of America, *Proceedings of the 1911 Annual Convention* (Indianapolis: Hollenbeck, 1911), p. 543.

4. David Brody, *Labor in Crisis: The Steel Strike of 1919* (Philadelphia: J. P. Lippincott, 1965), p. 15; Paul Douglas, *Real Wages in the United States, 1890-1926* (Boston:Houghton Mifflin, 1930), pp. 142, 154.

5. *See* appendix K.

6. Garraty, "United States Steel Corporation," p. 4.

7. Quoted in John Fitch, "Wear and Tear of the Twelve Hour day," *Survey*, March 5, 1921, p. 78.

8. John Fitch, "Some Pittsburgh Steel Workers," *Survey*, January 2, 1909, p. 557.

9. Ibid., p. 555.

10. Charles Walker, *Diary of a Furnace Worker* (Boston: Atlantic Monthly, 1922), p: 151.

11. Interview with Jack Pfeifer, in David Saposs, "Interviews with Steel Workers, Done during the Summer of 1920," deposited at the Wisconsin State Historical Society (hereafter cited as Saposs, "Interviews with Steel Workers").

12. Quoted in Hamlin Garland, "Homestead and Its Perilous Trades," *McClures Magazine* 11 (June 1894):9.

13. Crystal Eastman, *Work Accidents and the Law* (New York: Charities Publication Committee, 1910), p. 25.

14. James Forbes, "The Reverse Side," in Paul Kellogg, *Wage Earning Pittsburgh* (New York: Charities Publication Committee, 1914), pp. 313-25.

15. Eastman, *Work Accidents and the Law*, p. 26.

16. U.S. Immigration Comission, *Reports of the Immigration Commission* (Washington, D.C.: Government Printing Office, 1911), 8:18, 48 (hereafter cited as U.S. Immigration Commission).

17. Interview with Andy Tinko and Mike Urbian, in Saposs, "Interviews with Steel Workers."

18. Herbert Gutman, "Work, Culture and Society in Industrializing America," *American Historical Review* 78 (June 1973):553.

19. F. Zaneicki and W. I. Thomas, *The Polish Peasant in Europe and America* (New York: Gorham, 1927), 2:220. In Europe 65 percent of the immigrant steelworkers had been peasants; 12 percent of them had been artisans. U.S. Immigration Commission, 8:41.

20. E. P. Thompson, "Time, work, Discipline and Industrial Capitalism," *Past and Present* 38 (1967):56-97.

21. Anonymous letter dated June 6, 1909, in Zaneicki and Thomas, *Polish Peasant*, 2:273.

22. Interview with Mr. Stark, in Saposs, "Interviews with Steel Workers."

23. United States Steel Corporation, Bureau of Safety, Relief, Sanitation and Welfare, *Bulletin 4* (November 1913):45; Gerd Korman, "Americanization at the Factory Gate," *Industrial and Labor Relations Review* 18 (1965):72-96.

24. *Quincy* (Illinois) *Labor News*, October 7, 1911; Louis Farina, "The Call of the Steel Workers," *International Socialist Review* (August 1913): 77; Margaret Byington, *Homestead: Households of a Mill Town* (New York: Charities Publication Committee, 1910), p. 52.

25. Quoted in *New York World*, February 25, 1912.

26. U.S. Immigration Commission, 8:83.

27. Quoted in Alois B. Koukol, "A Slav's a Man for All That," in Paul Kellogg. *Wage Earning Pittsburgh* (New York: Charities Publication Committee, 1913), p. 67.

28. *New York World*, February 25, 1912.

29. Ibid.

30. Ibid.

31. Ibid.

32. Garraty, "United States Steel versus Organized Labor," p. 26; *see* appendix B for wage statistics.

33. Paul Kellogg, "The McKees Rocks Strike," *Survey*, October 9, 1909, p. 656. *See also* David Montgomery, *Workers Control in America* (Cambridge: University Press, 1979), pp. 91-112.

35. Quoted in Rufus Smith, "Some Phases of the McKees Rocks Strike," *Survey*, October 9, 1909, p. 38.

36. For a description and analyses of the McKees Rocks strike, *see* John Ingham, "A Strike in the Progressive Era," *Pennsylvania History* 90 (July 1966): 344-61; Melvyn Dubofsky, *We Shall Be All: A History of the Industrial Workers of the World* (Chicago: Quadrangle, 1969), pp. 198-208; and Philip Foner, *The Industrial Workers of the World* (New York: International, 1965), pp. 282-95.

37. *New York Call*, August 29, 1909; *Industrial Worker* (Spokane), August 27, 1909.

38. *Industrial Worker*, December 8, 1909, as quoted in Philip Foner, *Industrial Workers of the World*, p. 136.

39. *Chicago Socialist*, August 24, September 9, 1909.

40. Qutoed in *Amalgamated Journal*, August 26, 1909.

41. Dubofsky, *We Shall Be All*, pp. 206-208.

42. Foner, *Industrial Workers of the World*, p. 300; *Newcastle Free Press*, September 29, October 5, 1909.

43. U.S. Commissioner of Labor, *Report on the Strike at the Bethlehem Steel* (Washington, D.C.: Government Printing Office, 1910), p. 22.

44. Ibid., pp. 1-78; Graham Brooks, *The Age of Industrial Violence* (New York: Columbia University Press, 1966), p. 192.

45. Quoted in *American Federationist*, June 10, 1910, p. 504.

46. Appendix O.

47. Pennsylvania Secretary of State, *Smull's Legislative Handbook* (Harrisburg: State Printers, 1908), pp. 497-546; *see* appendix M. I am confining my election analysis to Pennsylvania's steel communities. Steel was produced in Illinois, Ohio, Indiana, New York, and Alabama, but most steel communities in these states had steelworker populations of less than 10 percent. It would therefore be almost impossible to identify how these men voted.

48. Victor Berger, "Classes in Free America," *Social Democratic Herald*, January 13, 1906.

49. *Newcastle Free Press*, November 11, 1909.

50. Socialist Party of America, "Elected Officials," Socialist Party Collection, Duke University.

51. *Newcastle Free Press*, June 29, 1912.

52. Ibid.

53. Ibid., November 4, 1911.

54. *New York World*, February 25, 1912.

55. Pennsylvania Secretary of State, *Smull's Legislative Handbook* (Harrisburg: State Printers, 1913), pp. 467-665. On the surface, it may appear as if the vote for Theodore Roosevelt, whose Progressive party was accused of stealing the Socialist platform, can be interpreted as an expression of steelworker radicalism. However, the 30 percent of the vote that Roosevelt received in the steel communities of the Pittsburgh district just about equaled his support in Pennsylvania as a whole and therefore cannot be invested with too much significance.

56. National Archives, "Manuscript Census," 1900. According to my calculation, in 1912 voter turnout was about 68 percent. In these sixty-one steel communities, 40,076 of an approximately 60,000 eligible voters went to the polls. These figures are based on a total population of 400,900, one-half of whom were immigrant and did not qualify for citizenship. This left 200,000 citizens. With an average family size of five and one-third of the steelworkers unmarried, there were approximately 60,000 adult males who qualified for the franchise. The population statistics were calculated from U.S. Department of Commerce, Bureau of the Census, "Population of Minor Civil Divisions, 1910," *Census of Population* (Washington, D.C.: Government Printing Office, 1914), 3:377-89; statistics on number of immigrants, family size, and unmarried steelworkers are found in U.S. Immigration Commission, *Reports of*

the *Immigration Commission* (Washington, D.C.: Government Printing Office, 1911), 8:107-39.

57. Wards adjacent to the steel mills were identified from street maps found in the Pennsylvania Historical Society (Philadelphia); ibid.

58. *Smull's Legislative Handbook, 1891-1917*; "Manuscript Census," 1900, appendix P.

59. E. H. Gary before the Lehigh Club, quoted in the *Iron City Journal* (Pittsburgh), February 23, 1912.

60. Quoted in Ida Tarbell, *The Life of Elbert Gary* (New York: Houghton Appleton, 1925), p. 156.

61. Garraty, "United States Steel versus Organized Labor," p. 6.

62. George Perkins to George Wickersham, February 23, 1909, George Perkins Papers, Columbia University.

63. Quoted in John Fitch, "Some Pittsburgh Steel Workers," *Survey*, January 2, 1909, p. 555.

64. Speech delivered by E. H. Gary on October 19, 1911, in "Addresses and Statements by E. H. Gary," bound and collected by the New York Public Library.

65. William Dickson, *American Iron and Steel Institute Yearbook, 1910*, p. 57; American Iron and Steel Institue, *Monthly Bulletin* (September 1913):241.

66. U.S. Steel, Bureau of Safety, Relief, Sanitation and Welfare, *Bulletin 3* (August 1912):48.

67. U.S. Steel, Bureau of Safety, Relief, Sanitation and Welfare, *Bulletin 4* (November 1913); *Bulletin 7* (December 1918):33.

68. For a detailed account of the corporation's welfare program, *see* U.S. Steel, Bureau of Safety, Relief, Sanitation and Welfare, *Bulletins 1-15* (1911-1925); U.S. Commissioner of Corporations, *Report of the Commissioner of Corporations on the Steel Industry* (Washington, D.C.: Government Printing Office, 1911), 1:330-32.

69. Appendixes B and C.

70. Dickson quoted in John Fitch, *The Steel Workers* (New York: Charities Publicaton Committee, 1910), p. 325; Cook quoted in *American Iron and Steel Institute Yearbook*, 1910, p. 69.

71. *Party Builder of the Socialist Party*, November 15, 1913; *Newcastle Free Press*, October 5, 26, November 2, 1912.

72. Appendix O.

73. Interview with Jack Pfeifer (former president of the McKeesport local of the Socialist party) in Saposs, "Interviews with Steel Workers"; James Weinstein, *The Decline of Socialism in America* (New York: Random House, 1967); and David Shannon, *The Socialist Party in America* (Chicago: Quadrangle, 1958).

74. Interview with Mr. Jenkins and Mike Connolly, in Saposs, "Interviews with Steel Workers."

75. Interview with C. C. Robinson of Donora, Pennsylvania, in Saposs, "Interviews with Steel Workers."

76. Brody, *Labor in Crisis*, p. 113.

77. Interview with C. C. Lane and Mr. Gibbons of Braddock, Pennsylvania, in Saposs, "Interviews with Steel Workers."

78. Estimate in William Z. Foster, *The Great Steel Strike and Its Lessons* (New York: B. W. Huebsch, 1920), pp. 156-60.

79. Appendix O.

80. *See* appendixes B and C. Brody points out that wages were reduced in 1921, but he does not call attention to the fact that by 1923 the average steelworker was again earning $1,640 a year and thus had about as much purchasing power as he had in 1919 or 1920.

The Nonunion Coalfields:
Violence, Socialism, and
Accommodation Again

Writing about class consciousness that never emerged or about class consciousness that flared up and quickly died inevitably involves essentially unsatisfactory "what might have beens." However, in the nonunion coalfields of Westmoreland County, Pennsylvania, and Kanawha County, West Virginia,[1] the "what might have beens," continued to be during the 1910s. The violent strikes that took place in these regions were as bloody as the conflicts described in previous chapters. Again, class conflict created Socialist sentiment, but only temporarily.

Before this dialectic of conflict and accommodation worked itself out, conditions in Westmoreland and Kanawha counties were strikingly similar to those that had existed in the Central Competitive Field prior to 1897 or, and more accurately, the anthracite mines of the early 1900s. Most of Westmoreland County's coking coal mines were owned by the U.S. Steel Corporation, whose executive board chairman, E. H. Gary, was often quoted as saying that "welfare was a simple duty that industry owed labor."[2] Conditions there, nevertheless, were almost identical to those that existed in the collieries of southern Appalachia where owners viewed the National Civic Federation ideal as being almost subversive.

The bankers and lawyers who sat on U.S. Steel's executive board were not about to make any concessions to the men who worked in the corporation's coal production subsidiaries unless they were forced to do so. Unorganized, these workers were in no position to force such concessions. The United Mine Workers had had no success in extending its 1897 victory in the Central Competitive Field to Westmoreland County, which was then the private preserve of Henry Clay Frick and Andrew Carnegie. Westmoreland County work days were two hours longer; the miners were paid 25 percent less.[3] Using tactics perfected in battles with the steelworkers, Frick broke all strikes by importing strikebreakers and Pinkerton detectives. Labor-management relations were unaffected by the 1901 merger that made the Henry Clay Frick Coal and Coke Company part of U.S. Steel.

During the next decade, conditions further deteriorated. Nineteenth-century miners had enjoyed some independence because of their skills, but mechanization had come quickly to the U.S. Steel's coal-producing subsidiaries. With their skills obsolete and without union protection, the Westmoreland County miners were soon completely at the mercy of their foremen. By 1910, the area was ripe for rebellion. Here, as in the coalfields of West Virginia where the UMW had also been defeated in 1897, the left-wing Socialist dream of radicalization through class conflict seemed to have a chance.

The men of Westmoreland County sensed all the dimensions of their exploitation. Frank Littlewood well articulated their grievances:

For the last five years, prior to 1910, conditions in Westmoreland county have been getting worse from day to day. I am a coal miner. I have been one all my life. In 1905, the company paid the miner 69.5¢ for a wagon that contained one and one-half tons of coal. From 1905 to 1910 wages for the same wagon have fallen to 53¢, while in the Pittsburgh district they have gone over that in percentage advance.[4]

Littlewood and his fellow workers, like their union counterparts, were supposed to be paid for "dead work," work that prepared a colliery for the actual mining of coal. Usually, however, nonunion miners were not paid for bailing water

or cutting through walls of slate. Without the UMW to protect
them, miners who felt cheated could only complain to a sympathetic Socialist press. The *Chicago Socialist* quoted R. C. Kelley:

When we come to a bit of slate in the coal we had to work through
it without any pay. I have worked for five or six hours at a vein of
slate, using as much as a stick of dynamite to loosen it, and for that
time I got nothing. We were paid only for the actual coal we mined
and we were cheated at that.[5]

Kelley might so speak to the editor of the *Chicago Socialist*,
but he would not dare complain to his foreman. In nonunion
coal mines workers perceived as troublemakers were summarily dismissed or assigned to an area of the colliery where it
was impossible to dig enough coal to earn a living. Men like
Frank Littlewood felt trapped in their black holes:

I have worked when I have not seen the light of day for 13 or 14 days [he
declared]. I have worked Sunday of late years. In the summertime the
trade fell off, but I worked for 13 years and never saw the light of day in
the wintertime many times in the last 25 years I have worked there and I
have been to work on Sunday. I was threatened I could just bring out my
tools if I didn't work on Sunday there would be no work for me on
Monday.[6]

Twelve years after the miners of the Central Competitive
Field had won the right to live and shop where they pleased,
nonunion coal miners still lived in company towns, with housing, stores, and even medical care obtainable only from the
company. The complaints were the same as those of the bituminous and anthracite miners earlier. "We had to deal with
the company store," declared one miner as late as 1911. "If
we did not we would be discharged."[7] Twenty-five percent
of a miner's wage went to the company for his house, but
even then his house was hardly his castle. The operators not
only owned the houses but all the land around them. They
believed they had the right to tell their men what visitors they
could or could not receive, especially if the visitor was a union
official. The operators hired private armies of mine guards

to enforce their property rights. These men not only physically intimidated the miners but compiled blacklists with great efficiency. Any man who attended a union meeting was not only dismissed but frequently shot at or beaten.[8]

Nonunion coal miners quite literally had to work under the gun. One miner, a man named Davie Jones, asserted that it was

common to find on pay day that ten dollars had been taken from your pay envelope. If you kicked up they promised to look the matter up. Tell you to return the next day. The next day they would have some of their Baldwin guards waiting for you. They would get hold of you and throw you out of the store, and tell you what they would do if you ever came up with a complaint again.[9]

Inez Smith, a miner's wife, had a similar experience. "My husband can't read and I took his statement to the store to have it corrected," she recalled. "I asked the bookkeeper to correct it. A mine guard got me by the arm and said, 'You get the hell out of here, we never make mistakes.' "[10]

The mine guards also managed to intimidate the leadership of the UMW. The union's organizers, though backed by a membership of 350,000, did not dare venture into the nonunion coalfields. Francis Freehan, the Socialist president of the Pittsburgh district, often tried to persuade the union's national administration to launch an organizing drive in Westmoreland County. John Mitchell, however, felt such a campaign would prove too costly.

The UMW, as it turned out, did not become involved in Westmoreland County until the late winter of 1910-1911 when the miners themselves took the initiative and began to organize. The impetus for the campaign came in January when U.S. Steel ordered the miners to begin using safety lamps and safety powder, measures that cost the miners money. "I had been working in that mine and I could make five wagons with naked light," one miner claimed, "but it took one wagon a day off when they put the safety lights on. I reduced my wages that much."[11]

Had grievance procedures long established in the unionized coalfields existed in Westmoreland County, the problem of safety devices might well have been quickly solved. In the unionized coalfields contracts specified that miners and operators should share the cost of safety equipment. The Westmoreland mines' management wanted no such sharing. On March 1, about 600 miners met at Greensburgh, Pennsylvania, to discuss their grievances. Management suspected that this gathering, which was attended by UMW vice-president Van Bittner, was being held for the purpose of organizing a union. Therefore, mine foremen were stationed outside the meeting hall with instructions to fire any man seen entering or leaving. Two hundred and thirty men were summarily discharged.[12]

So angered were the men by such treatment that Van Bittner soon had a local established. The new union drew up a list of grievances, with the miners demanding that the coal companies rehire the discharged men, pay according to union scale, adopt an eight-hour day, and recognize the UMW as the bargaining agent for the Westmoreland County miners. Management ignored these demands, and the strike began on March 15, 1910.

The battles that took place in Westmoreland County in 1910-1911 were reminiscent of those that had taken place in the Central Competitive Field in 1894 and in the anthracite region in 1902. In the middle of March, with 15,000 of the county's 20,000 miners walking the picket lines, the coal companies, with the help of the county sheriff, began evicting the strikers from their homes. "When the men did go on strike, the first thing that the coal operators did was rush a lot of deputies into the coal fields to kick the people and their furniture out on the streets," one angry miner declared. "When the deputies moved the furniture of the miners out on the streets, they went about it with Winchester rifles, a club and a revolver. They smashed the people's furniture on the street and the men and women who asked them to be careful got smashed in the head or kicked in the stomach."[13]

During the strike, the constabulary, paid, housed, and fed by U.S. Steel, killed one miner every five days. Each murder added to the tension in the region.[14] On July 3, when a deputy who was escorting strikebreakers home from work shot and killed the miners' popular leader, Jacob Putley, the county threatened to explode. The *United Mine Workers Journal* described the mood of the men:

Following the threats of lynching heard yesterday . . . miners have broken into bitter abuse of those who have made the deplorable conditions which exist in the Irwin field possible. . . . Putley's death has aroused the miners as they have never been aroused before. Mutterings, threats of revenge, are heard on every side, and even the arrogant, domineering coal companies are deeply concerned over the grave aspects of the situation.[15]

The threats of lynching were real. The county sheriff had to guard his deputy day and night. When tensions abated, strikers took to the highways with songs of industrial freedom.

Abe Lincoln said in sixty-one "the Negro must
be free"
And yet the miners in the Irwin field are kept
in slavery,
We rebelled against the tyranny, no more their
slaves we'll be,
We are fighting for industrial freedom.

Our employers on election day compelled us to
support
For Congress and the State Senate men who cut
our throats;
No more will they deceive us, no more will they
get our votes,
We are fighting for political freedom.

The infamous state constabulary have been
working day and night,
With deputies, thugs, assassins to break the
miners' strike,
They've murdered, jailed and evicted us, and
still we're in the fight,
Shouting the battle cry of freedom.[16]

These singing demonstrations were peaceful but effective. Miners, passing a working colliery, often found they could persuade strikebreakers to drop their tools and join the march. The operators responded by obtaining an injunction against public assemblage on the county's highways. Yet the marches continued. Deputy sheriff efforts to break them up inevitably led to violence.[17]

In Westmoreland County, U.S. Steel was long accustomed to operating as if it were both the government and the law. Upon arrest, strikers were not taken to jail but to the offices of the coal company where, handcuffed and chained, they waited for their foremen to decide their cases. If jail was ordered, the courts obliged with a sentence.[18]

Politics again became important. The *United Mine Workers Journal*, which was smuggled into the strikers' homes, pleaded with the men to take political action:

Remember that the judges and the sheriffs are not Gods. They hold their positions because of the dense ignorance of the workingman. Miners of Westmoreland county, use your ballots hereafter as you strike, turn out of office all the unfair, rotten officials, whether they are judges or sheriffs. Put the friends of the working class in the office.[19]

In Westmoreland County, the Socialists were the only friends the miners had. When strikers found it impossible to rent a meeting hall, the Socialists made their South Greensburgh headquarters available. During the sixteen-month strike, union meetings were held in this building almost every day. Whenever a strike rally was held, Socialist speakers would share the platform with union men. They told the miners that the behavior of the state police proved that the governor and the sheriff were "tools of the bosses," an argument that made an impression.[20] In November 1910, John W. Slayton, the party's candidate for governor, received 25 percent of the vote in Westmoreland County's seventy-three coal towns. Slayton was a traditional Marxist who sought to translate class conflict into Socialist electoral victories. In Westmoreland County, he capitalized on violent industrial conflict in order

to enlist workers in the fight for socialism. Table 6.1 shows
how successful he was in this effort. In November 1910, the
Socialists swamped the Democrats and did almost as well
as the Republicans. They probably would have done even
better if the dissenting vote had not been split by the Keystoners,
a group of reform-minded Democrats who publicly condemned
the behavior of the county sheriff. As in the anthracite coal
strike of 1902, the Keystoners largely appealed to native-born
coal miners; the Slavs and Italians tended to vote Socialist.[21]

Table 6.1
VOTE FOR GOVERNOR IN THE SEVENTY-THREE COAL TOWNS
OF WESTMORELAND COUNTY, 1910

Republican	Democrat	Socialist	Keystone
2,467	1,102	2,399	3,628

These returns were particularly impressive since two-thirds
of the Slavic and Italian miners, the groups toward whom the
Socialist party looked for its most reliable support, were disenfranchised aliens. Moreover, the 20,000 Westmoreland
County miners, scattered over a 1,600-square-mile area, were
often out of reach of the Socialists, who had limited resources
for campaigning. In towns where the party was able to conduct a sustained campaign the results were spectacular, at
least for American socialism. In West Latrobe, for example,
Slayton received 65 of 80 votes cast. In Saxman he was named
on 119 of 150 ballots, and in South Greensburgh he got 97
of 187 votes.[22]

Neither Socialist sentiment nor Socialist votes, however,
could win a strike, nor could the more than $1 million that
the UMW spent on the conflict. Refusing to compromise for
sixteen months, U.S. Steel finally, in June 1911, forced the
Westmoreland County miners back to work. Bitter over their
defeat, the men, unlike the successful strikers in the anthracite region and the Central Competitive Field, continued to

vote for socialism. In November 1911, the Socialists elected city councilmen, constables, school board members, and justices of the peace in South Greensburgh, Youngwood, Crestline, Wheaton, Derry, Irwin, and Trafford. A year later, Socialist presidential candidate Eugene Debs received 23 percent of the vote in the county's coal towns. As table 6.2 shows, in 1912, William Howard Taft and his usually successful Republican party were swamped, receiving only 2,082 of 15,115 votes cast. That year, the Socialists tied the Democrats and ran ahead of Theodore Roosevelt's popular and supposedly radical Bull Moose party.[23]

Table 6.2
VOTE FOR PRESIDENT IN THE SEVENTY-THREE COAL TOWNS
OF WESTMORELAND COUNTY, 1912

Republican	Democrat	Progressive	Socialist
2,082	4,620	3,833	4,620

The Socialists continued to do well in Westmoreland County until the party was shattered by government persecution during World War I. In 1916, at a time when the party was generally on the defensive, its candidate for president, Allen Benson, received 16 percent of the coal town vote in Westmoreland County. This represented 400 percent more support than that which he received in the steel towns of the nearby Pittsburgh district. The Socialists probably received many of these votes because they continued fighting for the Westmoreland County miners long after the UMW had abandoned the cause. Westmoreland miners did not stop voting Socialist until 1918 when, with Eugene Debs in jail for violating the wartime espionage act and with many Socialist newspapers banned from the mails, the party found it impossible to mount any kind of campaign.[24]

The UMW's abandonment of Westmoreland County was less than traumatic for the union since coking coal did not usually compete with the product of the unionized fields.

In West Virginia, however, the union could not retire from the fray so easily. The West Virginia problem had haunted the Joint Conference since 1898. Cheap West Virginia coal constantly undersold the Central Competitive Field. By 1912, West Virginia had become the largest coal-producing state in the nation. Almost 30 percent of the coal consumed in the midwest was dug in that state's nonunion mines. Clause 8 of the historic Joint Conference agreement had pledged the UMW to organize the West Virginia miners. The union, however, had never made a real effort to deliver on this promise, and the operators were not above using West Virginia as a bludgeon against the union. At the 1912 Joint Conference, the operators swung the club with full force.

We ask [a Senate committee on labor recorded them as saying] for the fulfillment of the pledge of 1898 upon which we made to the miners so many important and costly concessions. Though that promise has not been kept, we continued for twelve years to make additional concessions, by increasing the mining rate from 66¢ agreed upon at the time to 90¢ and in other respects conceding demands without any compensating concessions on the part of the miners, until we find ourselves at the limit of our financial safety.[25]

Whatever excuses the UMW might offer for the failure of its organizing efforts in West Virginia, such excuses did not meet the operators' competitive problem. The dedicated Socialist Adolph Germer analyzed its effect on collective bargaining:

West Virginia has always been a barrier to our progress. In every interstate Joint Conference between miners and operators the latter have always raised West Virginia as the battle cry against our demands. The vast amount of non-union coal that is mined in that state for practically nothing has made vast inroads in the markets that rightfully belong to the Central Competitive Field. We have reached the limit of our progress in the way of higher wages and better conditions.[26]
conditions.[26]

Germer very well might have been right, but the UMW had been hard put to do anything about it. Armed mine guards, patroling the narrow and isolated valleys of southern Appalachia, continued to discourage union organizers. The only area in which the UMW had had any success was along Kanawha County's Cabin Creek. There 2,500 union men managed to form a local and force the operators to grant them de facto recognition. However, in April 1912 when the Cabin Creek contract expired, the coal mine owners, not wanting to set any precedent for West Virginia's 60,000 nonunion miners, refused to renegotiate. On April 18, the Cabin Creek miners struck. They were soon joined by the nonunion men of nearby Paint Creek. Within a few days, almost all the collieries in the county were shut down. "The people were glad to come out," the wife of one striker remembered almost sixty years later. "They [the union] were giving us in provisions when we struck as much as we got when we were working. And now at least we had hope."[27]

As soon as the strike began, the operators, like their counterparts in Westmoreland County not long before, reinforced their private armies of mine guards. Again, miners were beaten and otherwise intimidated.[28] "People were afraid to speak, afraid of being killed," a miner and his wife recalled years afterward. "The thugs had the guns. The miners didn't have a chance."[29] Evictions from company-owned houses were carried out with brutality. Agnew and Artie Thomas well remembered the process: "We had no notice to get out; when we didn't the thugs just carried out our possessions into the creek bar. I saw people live there for two or three weeks. No use to protest, the coal companies were the government that ruled Charleston."[30] The miners and their families had to pick up their belongings and move into tent colonies.

The quickness and ferocity of the operators' action caught the miners off guard during the early days of the strike, but it did not take the strikers long to respond. West Virginia miners, who often hunted rabbits for food, knew how to use guns. They readily listened when Mother Jones, the UMW's most indefatigable organizer at age eighty-two, told them to "arm yourselves, return home and kill every god damned mine guard on these creeks."[31] Their mastery of firearms gave the West Virginia miners an edge over their militant

Slavic and Italian comrades in Pennsylvania. Ready fingers on triggers promised real violence once tempers grew hot enough. One Cabin Creek miner found words for the sentiments of many:

Conditions such as prevail here are a disgrace! The like of them does not prevail in any civilized country. I have never had to kill a man, and I hope I never will be compelled to kill one, but I would kill a dozen mine guards as I would kill so many rats, if they attempt to lord it over us as they are accustomed to do. And I would do it with a perfectly clear conscience.[32]

So in Kanawha County at least, the class struggle that William D. Haywood's IWW was counting on to radicalize the working class intensified. Armed strikers took to the hills and began to shoot at the mine guards who patroled the valleys below. The sniping frightened the mine guards but not enough to stop their defense of strikebreakers. As a result, on September 1, the miners took the battle to the mine guards' headquarters at Mucklow. That evening, a group of strikers loaded a box car with dynamite and started rolling it toward the tipple house where the mine guards lived. The guards managed to derail the box car before its deadly cargo exploded. Frustrated but undaunted, the strikers kept the guards under fire for thirty-six hours. Their mountain marksmanship took a toll of sixteen without losing a single man of their own.[33]

Governor William Glasscock, who thought that the operators had the conflict under control, declared martial law immediately after Mucklow. The miners, unaware of the role of militia in earlier strikes, welcomed the soldiers as protection against mine guards. They were suspicious enough, nevertheless, to hide their firearms rather than surrender them to the militia.[34] Their suspicions were soon enough confirmed. The troops stood by as mine guards smashed picket lines and arrested any striker who protested. Faced with overwhelming force, the strikers bided their time. Their wait was long, but their spirits remained militant. One striker told a reporter:

Hell is going to break loose here as soon as the troops are recalled unless the mine guards go at the same time. They have it in for us and we have it in for them. As soon as the troops go out, we fellows who have been working to unionize this region are going to catch it. But when they start something the fur will begin to fly.[35]

After six weeks of seeming peace, the militia withdrew, though many of its members signed up with the mine guards upon release from active duty. The strikers went on the offensive. By mid-November, they had complete control of the strike area. Governor Glasscock reimposed martial law. The militia marched in again. The strikers took to the hills, and in January with peace evidently restored, the militia withdrew once more.[36]

The guerrilla warfare quickly resumed. The mine guards outfitted an armored car, aptly called the Bull Moose Special, for an overwhelming blow at the strikers' tent colony in Holly Grove. Forewarned, the miners left their headquarters and set up ambush for the armored train. Taken by surprise, the mine guards lost sixty-eight men. Even so, they managed to regroup and keep the strikers from returning to the tent colony. After a while, the miners tried to pull out, but seventy-five of them were arrested by the state militia, which had been hurriedly mobilized.[37]

This time the appearance of the militia did not bring a lull in the fighting. Miners from all over Kanawha County poured into the area around Holly Grove intent on destroying the infamous Bull Moose Special. The militia imprisoned hundreds of them in a makeshift "bull open" on charges of conspiracy to commit murder.[38] Known Socialists became prime targets for the militia. Party headquarters was invaded and its occupants summarily rousted off to the bullpen. The offices of the *Socialist and Labor Star* and the *Charleston Labor Argus*, though outside the martial law zone, were raided and their presses smashed. The soldiers arrested the editor of the *Argus*, but the *Star*'s editor managed to escape to Kentucky.[39]

The Socialists were targets because they had gone all out for the strike. Most of the union organizers who came to West Virginia with UMW vice-president Frank Hayes were Socialists. Local party people also attended the union's meetings and rallies. These men and women, who had been trying unsuccessfully for so long to bring socialism to the miners, felt new hope. Many of them were followers of the IWW's William Haywood who had just been removed from the Socialist party's Executive Committee for allegedly advocating violence and sabotage. The Haywood supporters remained convinced that industrial warfare would radicalize the West Virginia miners. They purchased arms and joined the strikers in the assault on the Bull Moose Special. Frank Hayes looked on disapprovingly. For the moment though, faced with the militia, moderates and radicals worked in near harmony. Even Hayes, after facing the soldiers' callous brutality, had to concede the right of the miners to defend themselves.

During the strike, Socialists of all stripes tried to build the party and strengthen the union. They constantly told the miners, ''Boy don't stop until every man in your locality is a union man and a Socialist.''[40] The Socialists stressed to the miners how state and governmental officials worked with the operators to break the strike. Even the *United Mine Workers Journal* sounded more radical than it had in years:

How long [its editors asked the embattled miners] are we going to passively submit to legalized anarchy? When our homes are no longer sacred, our women no longer respected, and our lives no longer safe, it is time for serious thought and decided action. When a government does not protect the lives and liberties of its subjects, then the subjects owe nothing to the government. But the government is what the working class makes it. In the past, the working class had delegated the governmental power to the capitalist class and Paint Creek is an example of what we get, and as long as the workers delegate their political power to their masters just so long will they find the officials of the law on the side of their masters, but when the workers learn to vote and elect men of their class to make and execute laws, then the laws will be on the side of the workers and the officials will furnish them with protection.[41]

Mother Jones addressed the miners in a similar vein. When on August 13 a group gathered on the steps of the state capital to ask Governor Glasscock to disarm the mine guards, she declared, "The Governor was placed in this building by Scott and Elkins [coal barons] and he don't dare cross them. Therefore, you are asking the Governor to do something he cannot do without betraying the class he belongs to."[42]

The words of Mother Jones and the Socialists took hold. The West Virginia Socialists, like so many of their comrades in earlier strikes, now found that it was not difficult to teach the miners "the fundamentals of Socialism," since "the class struggle was clear and apparent" to the embattled strikers.[43] As retired miner, Artie Thomas, was to remember almost sixty years later, "Everybody wore Debs buttons because the state police was in league with the mine owners."[44]

The election returns show that Thomas's recollections were quite lucid. In November 1912, the Kanawha County miners gave Eugene Debs some 55 percent of their vote. The Socialist vote was so large because, unlike in other strife-torn areas, most Kanawha County miners were native-born Americans with the right and habit of voting. Thus, despite the fact that local Republicans and Progressives united behind William Howard Taft in order to meet the Socialist challenge, Eugene Debs received 2,328 votes, compared to 1,142 for Taft and 667 for Woodrow Wilson.[45] In direct response to the government's repression, the miners also elected a Socialist constable and a Socialist justice of the peace. The party almost captured the county's district attorney's and sheriff's offices. Only the voters of the city of Charleston saved the minions of law and order from that. The Socialist vote on Paint and Cabin Creeks stunned both the complacent Democrats and the more flexible Progressive Republicans, whose successful gubernatorial candidate, Henry Hatfield, had tried to appeal to the miners by criticizing Glasscock's use of the militia.

Although Hatfield's appeal had persuaded few miners to vote for him, once in office, he was able to drive a wedge between the UMW and the more radical West Virginia Socialists, who hoped that a continued intensification of the class struggle would permanently radicalize the miners. Much to the latter's chagrin, Hatfield's compromise strike settlement of May 1913 was accepted by both the union and the operators. It provided for a nine-hour day, semimonthly pay, and the rehiring of all strikers.

Most West Virginia Socialists thought the settlement a sell-out. Wyatt H. Thompson, editor of the *Socialist and Labor Star*, argued upon his return to Kentucky that the Hatfield compromise had robbed the miners of a real victory. He pointed out that the governor's proposals provided for neither the elimination of the mine guards nor for the recognition of the union. Angry at the UMW for having given up so much, Thompson accused the union of concealing the actual terms of the settlement from the miners.[46]

The West Virginia Socialists desperately tried to keep the strike going. Leaders of the UMW, outraged, accused the radicals of being irresponsible syndicalists. The Socialist party's national leadership, engaged in a determined struggle with the IWW, joined in the condemnation. In May of 1913, the National Executive Committee sent Eugene Debs, Victor Berger, and Adolph Germer to West Virginia to investigate conditions in the coalfields. After meeting with the governor, they endorsed his strike settlement, declared that he was making a good faith effort to restore civil liberties, and accused the critics of the Hatfield compromise of acting solely in order to undermine the United Mine Workers and promote the IWW. Eugene Debs called the West Virginia Socialists a "bunch of IWWites" who "had never done a particle of organizing in the dangerous districts of the state." He accused them of being the "real enemies of the working class."[47]

Debs's stand bewildered the West Virginia Socialists. They could not understand how he could ask them to trust Governor Hatfield, who, like his predecessor, still held hundreds of their comrades imprisoned. Some of the West Virginia Socialists concluded that Debs had become a mere "vote wooer, who did not wish to offend influential craft union leaders."[48]

The West Virginia Socialists were in fact in closer touch with rank-and-file workers and voters than was either the UMW or Debs. The strike settlement lasted only six weeks. In mid-June, the men walked off their jobs again, claiming discrimination against "union men." As the radicals had predicted, the bosses soon surrendered. They not only agreed to get rid of the mine guards but signed a contract with the UMW. The settlement was one that West Virginia Socialists could endorse.[49]

So the West Virginia Socialist party had been proven right and the UMW wrong, even on a point of bargaining. For a time the miners of the strife-torn area seemed to remember. In November 1914, the party's candidate for governor received 20 percent of the vote in Kanawha County, which meant that he must have been named on at least 50 percent of the ballots cast on Paint and Cabin Creeks. But even here, where industrial strife had been so violent and IWW involvement so great, radical sentiment soon faded. In 1916, Allen Benson, the Socialist candidate for president, received less than 1 percent of the vote in Kanawha County.[50] In contrast, the defeated Westmoreland County miners gave the Socialists 16 percent of their vote that year.

Peace and accommodation had come to West Virginia's Paint and Cabin Creeks. Elsewhere in the state, miners continued to work nonunion collieries. Not surprisingly, between 1919 and 1928 one bloody conflict after another erupted in the area. Miners, operators, mine guards, and militia reenacted the dialectic of violence in Kanawha County. In 1919, Logan County was the scene of bloody conflict. In 1920, federal troops were required to quell disturbances in Mingo County. In 1921 Logan erupted again, and in 1924, a bloody four-year strike began in Fairmount County. The Socialist party, now virtually moribund, was the only actor missing from the drama. In 1920, running for president from the Atlanta Penitentiary, Eugene Debs received only twenty-seven votes in bloody Logan County.[51]

Nor did the UMW, always half-foe and half-friend of the Socialists, fare much better in following years, During the 1920s, coal production in the nonunion southern Appalachian field increased fivefold. Operators of the Central Competitive Field saw their old nightmares become realities. By 1925, more than half of the nation's coal was being produced in nonunion collieries. The UMW tried refusing to permit wages to be reduced below a $7.50 scale agreed upon at a 1924 Jackson-ville, Florida, conference. At such rates, operators, trying to mine and sell union coal, had little chance in the market. Therefore, even though they had worked harmoniously with the UMW for decades, the operators concluded that they had to declare war. They broke the Jacksonville agreement and braced themselves for the inevitable conflict. The UMW called a strike. The operators once again brought in mine guards and strikebreakers. By the end of the decade, the UMW was all but destroyed. Its $7.50 scale was a memory. After the de-pression of 1929 hit the industry, miners, like their fathers of forty years before, were forced to work for $1.50 a day. Again, when reporters visited the coalfields, they saw "thou-sands of men, women and children literally starving to death."[52]

The miners were to react to the depression of the 1930s in much the same way as their fathers had responded to the crisis of the 1890s: they organized. When the UMW, led now by John L. Lewis, tried once again to organize all the coalfields, the response was overwhelming. Overjoyed organizers watched in awe as "the miners [moved] into the union en masse."[53] This time, even U.S. Steel and the men who owned mines in southern Appalachia succumbed before the union's onslaughts. In September 1933, a new Joint Contract was negotiated, which once again enabled miners to earn five dollars in an eight-hour day.

The accommodation was again timely. Just when it appeared as if the coal miners might become interested in the radical politics of a Communist party that was becoming active in the coal-fields, the miners' faith in the American system was restored. Many coal miners, organized in a union soon protected and legitimized by the Wagner Act, came to view the fatherly Franklin Delano Roosevelt as the personification of a newly reformed American political economy. "John L. Lewis and F.D.R., they were a team. They did an awful lot for this country. I don't care what they call Roosevelt—a Democrat or a Socialist, he was a great man," a retired miner would declare decades later. This man had dug coal in Kanawha County and voted for Eugene Debs in 1912. Fifty-six years later he found himself in the political mainstream. He no longer viewed West Virginia's police as a "bunch of thugs" but rather the "best law enforcement officers in the land."[54]

NOTES

1. Westmoreland County is east of Pittsburgh. Kanawha County is in northeastern West Virginia. In 1910 it produced about 25 percent of the state's coal.

2. Elbert H. Gary, "Address to Subsidiary Presidents," in *Addresses and Statements by E. H. Gary* (Cambridge: Business History Society), 2:256.

3. By 1910, most unionized coal miners earned between $2.00 and $2.50 for an eight-hour day. In Westmoreland County and in West Virginia, nonunion coal miners were paid $2.00 for a ten-hour day (*see* appendix Q).

4. U.S. Congress, House Committee on Rules, *Investigation of the Troubles in the Bituminous Coal Field of Westmoreland County, Pennsylvania* (Washington, D.C.: Government Printing Office, 1912), p. 7 (hereafter cited as House Rules, *Investigation Westmoreland*). By 1910, most unionized coal miners earned between $2.00 and $2.50 for an eight-hour day.

5. *Chicago Socialist*, September 21, 1910.

6. House Rules, *Investigation Westmoreland*, p. 52.

7. Miner quoted in *New York Call*, March 21, 1911; similar conditions existed in West Virginia; *see United Mine Workers Journal*, October 2, 1902 (hereafter cited as *UMWJ*); appendix Q.

8. *See* U.S. Commissioner of Labor, *Report on the Strike in the Bituminous Coal Fields in Westmoreland County, Pennsylvania* (Washington, D.C.: Government Printing Office, 1912), p. 89 (hereafter cited as Commissioner of Labor, *Report Westmoreland*; *see* testimony of Peter Cajano before U.S. Senate, Committee on Education and Labor, *Conditions in the Paint Creek Fields of West Virginia* (Washington, D.C.: Government Printing Office, 1913), p. 813 (hereafter cited as Senate Committee on Education and Labor, *Conditions in Paint Creek*).

9. Senate Committee on Education and Labor, *Conditions at Paint Creek*, p. 651.

10. Ibid., p. 650.

11. House Rules, *Investigation Westmoreland*, p. 51.

12. Commissioner of Labor, *Report Westmoreland*, p. 25.

13. Quoted in ibid., p. 79.

14. Ibid., pp. 33-39.

15. *UMWJ*, July 28, 1910, p. 4.

16. "Strikers Marching Song," in ibid., September 1, 1910, p. 3.

17. Commissioner of Labor, *Report Westmoreland*, pp. 84-85.

18. *UMWJ*, September 22, 1910, p. 1, June 22, 1911, p. 3; *Chicago Socialist*, September 1, 1910; House Rules, *Investigation Westmoreland*, p. 32.

19. *UMWJ*, September 1, 1910, p. 3.

20. Thomas Kennedy, "The Irwin Coal Strike," *International Socialist Review* (July 1910):202.

21. "Manuscript Census," 1900; Pennsylvania Secretary of State, *Smull's Legislative Handbook, 1912* (Harrisburg: State Printers, 1913), pp. 558-61. As in previous strike elections, voter turnout was quite high, about 70 percent. In Westmoreland County's seventy-three coal towns, 9,596 of approximately 13,000 adult male citizens went to the polls. Usually only about 55 percent of them did so. Voter turnout was calculated from a population statistic of 111,000 (50 percent of whom were immigrants who did not qualify for the franchise), average family size 4.7, with one-third of the coal miners unmarried. U.S. Department of Commerce, Bureau of the Census, "Population of Minor Civil Divisions, 1910," *Census of Population* (Washington, D.C.: Government Printing Office, 1914), 3:379-80; U.S. Immigration Commission, *Reports of the Immigration Commission* (Washington, D.C.: Government Printing Office, 1911), 1:21-121.

22. "Manuscript Census," 1900; Pennsylvania Secretary of State, *Smull's Legislative Handbook, 1912* (Harrisburg: State Printers, 1913), pp. 558-61; Socialist Party of America, "Elected Officials," Social Party Collection, Duke University.

23. Pennsylvania Secretary of State, *Smull's Legislative Handbook, 1913* (Harrisburg: State Printers, 1914), pp. 671-75.

24. Pennsylvania Secretary of State, *Smull's Legislative Handbook* (1915, 1916, 1917, 1918, 1919) (Harrisburg: State Printers, 1916-1920).

25. Senate Committee on Education and Labor, *Conditions at Paint Creek*, p. 2132.

26. Ibid., p. 1587.

27. Interview with Kathie Hackney, in James Axelrod, "Personal Interviews with Retired Coal Miners," tape recorded during the spring of 1970 (hereafter cited as "Axelrod's Interviews").

28. Interview with Jim and Rosa Austin, "Axelrod's Interviews";

Senate Committee on Education and Labor, *Conditions in Paint Creek*, pp. 360-1193.

29. Interview with Agnew and Artie Thomas in "Axelrod's Interviews."

30. Interview with Jim and Rosa Austin.

31. Quoted in Howard Lee, *Bloodletting in Appalachia* (Morgantown: University of West Virginia Press, 1969), p. 21.

32. Quoted in Harold West, "Civil War in the West Virginia Coal Mines," *Survey*, April 15, 1913, p. 45.

33. *Newcastle Free Press*, September 13, 1912; Fred Mooney, *Struggle in the Coal Fields: The Autobiography of Fred Mooney* (Morgantown: University of West Virginia Press, 1967), p. 34; Senate Committee on Education and Labor, *Conditions in Paint Creek*, p. 17.

34. Interview with Charlie Paine in "Axelrod's Interviews."

35. West, "Civil War," p. 48.

36. Mooney, *Struggle in the Coal Fields*, pp. 36-39; interview with Charlie Paine.

37. Ralph Chaplin, "Violence in West Virginia," *International Socialist Review* (April 1913): 733; Lee, *Bloodletting in Appalachia*, pp. 26-28.

38. Lee, *Bloodletting in Appalachia*, pp. 30-42.

39. Chaplin, "Violence in West Virginia," p. 735; David Corbin, *The Socialist and Labor Star* (Huntington, W. Va.: Appalachian Movement Press, 1972); David Corbin, "Betrayal in the West Virginia Coal Fields: Eugene V. Debs and the Socialist Party of America, 1912-1914," *Journal of American History* 64 (March 1978): 987-1009.

40. *UMWJ*. July 11, 1912, p. 2.

41. Ibid.

42. Quoted in Senate Committee on Education and Labor, *Conditions in Paint Creek*, p. 2263.

43. Edward Kintzer, "Miners Play a Waiting Game," *International Socialist Review* (November 1912): 391.

44. "Axelrod's Interviews."

45. *Wheeling Majority*, November 14, 1912.

46. Wyatt H. Thompson, "How a Victory Was Turned into a Settlement," *International Socialist Review* (May 1913): 12-17.

47. Quoted in James Weinstein, *The Decline of Socialism in America* (New York: Random House, 1969), pp. 34-35; E. O. McPherron to Adolph Germer, July 18, 1913, Germer Mss., Wisconsin State Historical Society.

48. Leslie Murray, "Hatfield's Challenge to the Socialist Party," *International Socialist Review* (June 1913): 881; Murray, "Union Repudiates

Debs Escorts Haggerty," *International Socialist Review* (July 1913): 22; Fred Merrick, "The Betrayal of the West Virginia Red Neck," *International Socialist Review*, (July 1913): 10.

49. Wyatt H. Thompson, "The War is Over," *International Socialist Review* (August 1913): 162; *UMWJ*, May 1, 1913, p. 2.

50. West Virginia Secretary of State, *West Virginia Blue Book, 1916* (Charleston: State Printers, 1917), p. 704.

51. Ibid., 1924, p. 672.

52. Irving Bernstein, *The Lean Years: A History of the American Workers, 1920-1933* (Boston: Houghton Mifflin, 1966), pp. 117-36.

53. Irving Bernstein, *The Turbulent Years: A History of the American Worker, 1933-1941* (Boston: Houghton Mifflin, 1971), pp. 37-77.

54. Interview with Charles Shipley and Bob Edwards in "Axelrod's Interviews."

Conclusion

The failure of American socialism was striking. During the early years of the twentieth century while European Socialists were electing hundreds of representatives to legislatures between 20 and 35 percent of the national suffrages, American Socialists were receiving 6 percent of the vote or less. Victor Berger of Milwaukee and Meyer London of New York were the only Socialists ever to sit in Congress.

Many European coal miners and steelworkers regularly voted Socialist, but their American counterparts for the most part cast ballots for socialism, if at all, only when the class struggle erupted in violence. Contrary to the expectations of Karl Marx and his American left-wing Socialist followers, such violent class struggle did not permanently radicalize American coal miners and steelworkers. Even in Kanawha County, West Virginia, where the state militia and the miners were locked in combat for more than a year, Socialist sentiment faded after the United Mine Workers was recognized.

In 1908, realizing that class conflict alone would not radicalize the working class, Eugene Debs left the Industrial Workers of the World. Thereafter, while still seeking to involve himself in the workers' struggles, he began to move toward the position of Victor Berger, who was placing his faith in political organization. Debs and Berger concluded that the European

Socialists owed their success to their superior political organizations and their intimate relationships with established trade unions. In 1913, hoping to cement such a relationship with the UMW, Debs publicly condemned the IWW for its attempt to undermine the settlement that the UMW had negotiated in West Virginia. Debs continued to seek involvement in the major coal and steel strikes of the period. He would never join Victor Berger in calling upon Socialists to work for "class understanding through the development of mutual class respect." Nevertheless, his behavior during the Kanawha County coal strike of 1912-1913 shows that when faced with a choice, he would align himself with an established trade union like the UMW. He refused to throw his prestige behind the IWW's efforts to radicalize the working class through class struggle.

The repudiation of the IWW must have seemed to Eugene Debs to have been the logical response to the tactics of the National Civic Federation. By 1900, men like Mark Hanna, George Perkins, and E. H. Gary had realized that to continue to be as uncompromising toward labor in the future as they had been in the past might permanently radicalize their employees. In effect, they set out to undercut the Socialist movement by blunting class conflict. They were determined not to permit the tactics of William Haywood and his IWW to succeed. Even so, as we have seen, there were two schools of thought within the NCF. Marcus Alonzo Hanna and the bituminous coal operators were convinced that it was necessary for them to recognize conservative trade unions, thereby encouraging the rank-and-file workers to follow the responsible leadership of Samuel Gompers and John Mitchell. George Perkins and E. H. Gary of the United States Steel Corporation, on the other hand, did not believe it necessary, at least in their industry, to recognize trade unions. These men, having seen Andrew Carnegie and Henry Clay Frick reduce the Amalgamated Association of Iron and Steel Workers to impotence, believed that "fair" wages and welfare capitalism would "make it certain that there would never be any excuse for the advancement of the ideas of the anarchist or the socialist."

This difference in approach appears to have been a response

to differing conditions in coal and steel. Even the most progressive capitalist rarely made any concession to his employees without being forced to do so. The bituminous coal operators were faced with a well-organized UMW and an industry plagued by cut-throat competition and overproduction. In 1897, they recognized the union, hoping that this would not only ensure labor peace but, by binding all operators to a fixed wage scale, make it impossible for any one of them to cut prices in order to undersell the competition. In contrast, the anthracite operators, in an oligopolistic industry, were able to resist the UMW, at least until 1902. Then the union, buoyed by its victory in the Central Competitive Field, forced them to bargain with it. In steel, Morgan, Gary, and Perkins of the dominant U.S. Steel combine were never challenged by a strong labor union; Frick and Carnegie had taken care of that before U.S. Steel was organized. If they had been faced with a union like the UMW, they might also have bargained as J. P. Morgan in fact did in anthracite coal.

When the crises came and it appeared as if class conflict would convert coal miners and steelworkers to socialism, capitalists responded as best they could. The four crises in labor-management relations here described were great turning points in the development of the American political economy, but they did not pave the way for a Socialist revolution or even for a strong Socialist movement. Instead they hastened the transition from a laissez-faire political economy, dominated by captains of industry who exploited labor without giving much thought to the long-range consequences of their behavior, to the twentieth-century system of corporate capitalism, dominated by sophisticated men who saw reform as the best insurance against revolution.

Could it have happened any differently, or did the dialectic of conflict and accommodation inevitably lead to a corporate capitalist synthesis? Could the IWW's dream of continually escalating class conflict resulting in a Socialist revolution have become a reality? Historians have traditionally argued that the United States's relatively high standard of living coupled with social and geographic mobility foreclosed this alternative.

However, in western Europe, where wages were lower and mobility more limited, the revolution also failed. True, powerful Socialist parties were forged by the conflicts of the early industrial period, but these organizations tended to become entrenched bureaucracies with vested interests in the electoral system and the status quo. As long as there was a theoretical possibility for socialism to come to power through the existing political structure and as long as the capitalist class was willing to compromie with workers' movements, Socialist leaders were unlikely to exhort the rank and file to the barricades. Of course, such a movement could have taken place spontaneously, but the evidence cited here indicates that while such eruptions may be violent and temporarily radicalize those who participate in them, once the immediate crises are over, there is a return to normal political behavior.

In Europe, this meant voting Socialist. In the United States, it meant voting for whichever Democratic or Republican politician posed as a friend of the working class. The result was almost the same: corporate capitalism and the welfare state. While European governments have nationalized some industries, these have tended to be failing enterprises that have no longer interested the capitalists. The bailout of the Chrysler Corporation may eventually take this form.

It appears that neither the west European nor the American model leads to Socialist revolution. What is needed is constant class conflict without a safety valve to relieve the pressure. Under normal circumstances few systems tolerate such conditions.

Appendices

Appendix A

DAILY WAGES IN IRON AND STEEL MILLS FOR SELECTED SKILLED AND UNSKILLED OCCUPATIONS, 1875-1890

Year	Puddlers	Rollers	Furnace Keepers	Fillers
1865	$3.42	$3.47	$1.71	$1.49
1876	2.96	3.53	1.67	1.37
1877	2.83	3.60	1.56	1.37
1878	3.04	4.39	1.36	1.37
1879	3.39	2.81	1.59	1.38
1880	3.35	5.07	1.62	1.56
1881	3.32	6.02	1.84	1.74
1882	3.06	4.78	1.95	1.88
1883	2.78	3.60	2.25	1.88
1884	2.55	3.15	2.02	1.65
1885	3.22	5.35	2.25	1.71
1886	2.76	3.38	2.05	1.71
1887	3.50	7.95	2.18	1.81
1888	3.20	3.72	2.04	1.61
1889	3.19	5.13	1.91	1.48
1890	3.29	3.97	2.02	1.67

Source: U.S. Department of Labor, Bureau of Labor Statistics, *Bulletin 604: History of Real Wages in the United States, from Colonial Times to 1928* (Washington, D.C.: Government Printing Office, 1932), pp. 241-50.

Appendix B

AVERAGE EARNINGS OF EMPLOYED WAGE EARNERS IN THE IRON AND STEEL INDUSTRY, 1892-1926

Year	Average Annual Wage
1892	$ 413
1893	400
1894	353
1895	373
1896	344
1897	357
1898	378
1899	434
1900	456
1901	470
1902	489
1903	501
1904	676
1905	492
1906	520
1907	544
1908	478
1909	517
1910	592
1911	592
1912	607
1913	718
1914	685
1915	684
1916	820
1917	1,012
1918	1,324
1919	1,487
1920	1,725
1921	1,331
1922	1,290
1923	1,533
1924	1,514
1925	1,569
1926	1,604

Source: Compiled from data provided by Paul Douglas, *Real Wages in the United States, 1890-1926* (Boston: Houghton Mifflin, 1930), p. 271, and in Albert Rees, *Real Wages in the United States* (Princeton: Princeton University Press, 1961), p. 61. I used Douglas's figures for hours worked but Rees's for hourly wages, since he, unlike Douglas, included sheet steel, tin plate, and hoop mill workers in his compilations.

Appendix C

THE COST OF LIVING, 1890-1926

Year	Cost of Living Index [a]
1890	104
1891	101
1892	102
1893	100
1894	97
1895	97
1896	99
1897	100
1898	100
1899	102
1900	106
1901	108
1902	111
1903	116
1904	115
1905	115
1906	119
1907	126
1908	121
1909	121
1910	128
1911	132
1912	133
1913	137
1914	139
1915	136
1916	149
1917	179
1918	218
1919	247
1920	286
1921	246
1922	229
1923	234
1924	234
1925	240
1926	241

Year	Cost of Living Index [b]
1890	91
1891	91
1892	91
1893	90
1894	86
1895	84
1896	84
1897	83
1898	83
1899	83
1900	84
1901	85
1902	86
1903	88
1904	89
1905	88
1906	90
1907	94
1908	92
1909	91
1910	95
1911	95
1912	97
1913	99
1914	100

Source: [a]Paul Douglas, *Real Wages in the United States, 1890-1926* (Boston: Houghton Mifflin, 1930), p. 60, for 1890-1899 = 100. [b]Figures compiled by the National Bureau of Economic Research. Albert Rees, *Real Wages in the United States, 1890-1914* (Princeton: Princeton University Press, 1961), p. 117, for 1914 = 100.

Measuring the movement in the cost of living is a difficult, if not impossible, task. For the 1890-1914 period two indexes are available: Paul Douglas's work done in 1930 and the data of the National Bureau of Economic Research, which were collected thirty-one years later. Both have their shortcomings. Douglas's work lacks a rent component. The NBER's data, however, have more serious deficiencies. The NBER underestimated the percentage of family income spent on food. Its figure of 44.1 percent might be accurate for a middle-class family, but Douglas's figure of 63.2 percent is closer to what a working-class family must have spent on food. The NBER took clothing prices from the Sears and Roebuck catalog, but few workers bought their clothing from Sears and Roebuck, and almost as few purchased clothing of any kind. Douglas's estimate of the cost of clothing based on prices of scoured wool, worsted yarn, and cotton measured by the yard is probably more accurate than the NBER's. When constructing a consumer price index for the 1890-1914 period, it is essential to weigh accurately a family's relative expenditure on food and clothing. During this period, while the price of food rose by 39 percent, the price of clothing fell by 26 percent. By overestimating the proportion of family income spent on purchased clothing, the NBER underestimated the rise in the cost of living. It estimated that it rose by 11 percent during the 1890-1914 period. Douglas's figure of 37 percent is probably more accurate. Therefore, I have used Paul Douglas's consumer price index throughout this book.

Appendix D
DEATHS AND INJURIES IN THE COAL MINES OF PENNSYLVANIA AND ILLINOIS

Year	Number of Employees per Life Lost	Number of Men per Injury
Pennsylvania		
1891	318	
1892	592	
1893	589	
1894	585	
1895	541	
1896	467	
1897	587	
Illinois		
1883	179.6	103.6
1884	556	129.8
1885	652	144.6
1886	497	151
1887	654	149
1888	716	164.3
1889	539	149.6
1890	549	97.2
1891	590	89.8
1892	573	91

Source: For Pennsylvania, U.S. Coal Commission, *Report* (Washington, D.C.: Government Printing Office, 1925), 1:28. For Illinois, Illinois Bureau of Labor Statistics, *Annual Report, 1895* (Springfield: State Printers, 1896), p. 486.

Appendix E

WAGES OF BITUMINOUS COAL MINERS, 1890-1897

Year	Average Daily Wage	Days Worked	Average Weekly Wage	Average Yearly Wage
1890	$1.80	226	$10.80	$406
1891	1.69	223	10.14	386
1892	1.79	219	10.74	392
1893	1.88	204	11.28	383
1894	1.71	171	10.26	292
1895	1.58	194	9.48	304
1896	1.47	192	8.82	282
1897	1.38	196	8.28	256

Source: Paul Douglas, *Real Wages in the United States* (Boston: Houghton Mifflin, 1930), p. 350.

Appendix F

RELATIVE REAL EARNINGS OF BITUMINOUS COAL MINERS, 1890-1897

Year	
1890	100
1891	95
1892	99
1893	98
1894	77
1895	81
1896	73
1897	69

Source: Paul Douglas, *Real Wages in the United States, 1890-1926* (Boston: Houghton Mifflin, 1930), p. 353.

TONNAGE RATES, 1893-1897

District	1893	1897
Pittsburgh	65-79¢/ton	47-54¢/ton
Illinois and Ohio	70-75¢/ton	45-51¢/ton

Source: Arthur E. Suffern, *Conciliation and Arbitration in the Coal Industry* (Boston: Houghton Mifflin, 1915), p. 41.

Appendix G

NUMBER AND DURATION OF ANTHRACITE AND BITUMINOUS COAL STRIKES, 1890-1894

Year	Strikes	establishments	Mine Days Closed	Strikers
Anthracite				
1890	7	9	510	8,224
1891	15	68	2,389	3,086
1892	6	6	163	1,016
1893	6	6	93	7,229
1894	9	9	161	1,826
Bituminous				
1890	19	36	8,599	35,548
1891	28	263	5,473	52,224
1892	21	43	6,095	10,478
1893	21	98	2,513	16,474
1894	22	547	43,122	73,434

Source: U.S. Commissionner of Labor, *Tenth Annual Report: Strikes and Lockouts (Washington, D.C.: Government Printing Office, 1895), pp. 1022-1137.*

Appendix H

WAGES IN THE BITUMINOUS COAL INDUSTRY, 1897-1920

Year	Days Worked	Average Daily Wage	Average Annual Wage
1897	196	$1.38	$ 270.48
1898	211	1.50	316.50
1899	234	1.62	379.08
1900	234	1.79	418.76
1901	225	2.02	474.70
1902	230	2.13	489.90
1903	225	2.32	522.00
1904	202	2.33	470.66
1905	211	2.37	500.07
1906	213	2.52	486.36
1907	234	2.48	580.30
1908	193	2.52	486.36
1909	209	2.51	524.59
1910	217	2.57	557.59
1911	211	2.62	542.82
1912	223	2.75	613.75
1913	232	2.72	631.04
1914	195	2.78	542.15
1915	203	2.90	588.70
1916	230	3.26	749.86
1917	243	4.02	976.86
1918	249	4.86	1,210.14
1919	195	5.63	1,097.75
1920	220	6.30	1,386.00

Relative Real Wages, 1890-1899 = 100			
1897	84	1900	103
1898	91	1901	114
1899	97	1902	117

Appendix H—*Continued*

Relative Real Wages, 1890-1899 = 100			
1903	122	1912	126
1904	123	1913	121
1905	126	1914	122
1906	129	1915	129
1907	120	1916	134
1908	127	1917	137
1909	126	1918	136
1910	122	1919	139
1911	121	1920	134

Source: Paul Douglas, *Real Wages in the United States, 1890-1926* (Boston: Houghton Mifflin, 1930), pp. 140-43.

Appendix I

WAGES IN THE ANTHRACITE COAL INDUSTRY, 1899-1920

Year	Days Worked	Average Daily Wage	Average Annual Wage
1899	152	$1.90	$ 290.98
1900	152	1.67	254.10
1901	196	1.92	362.30
1902	116	2.25	261.00
1903	206	2.38	480.28
1904	200	2.88	576.00
1905	215	2.43	527.45
1906	195	2.54	475.30
1907	220	2.60	572.00
1908	200	2.50	500.00
1909	205	2.44	490.20
1910	229	2.38	545.02
1911	246	2.32	570.72
1912	231	2.41	556.71
1913	257	2.31	593.67
1914	245	2.34	573.30
1915	230	2.63	604.90
1916	253	2.53	640.09
1917	285	3.22	806.76
1918	293	4.39	1,286.27
1919	266	5.11	1,355.26
1920	271	5.97	1,627.86

Source: Paul Douglas, *Real Wages in the United States, 1890-1926* (Boston: Houghton Mifflin, 1930), p. 154.

Appendix J

VOTE IN THE 1909 UNITED MINE WORKERS PRESIDENTIAL ELECTION

	District	Tom Lewis	John Walker
1	Anthracite region, Scranton Wilkes-Barre area, northern field	7,119	698
2	Central Pennsylvania (bituminous)	5,746	6,881
5	Pittsburgh district	2,972	6,938
6	Ohio	12,323	4,282
7	Anthracite region, Hazleton area, middle field	1,443	160
9	Anthracite region Schuylkill County, southern field		
10	Washington state	569	195
11	Indiana	1,370	7,324
12	Illinois	22,482 ½	25,337 ½
13	Iowa	6,937	2,580
14	Kansas	496	2,916
15	Colorado	412	406
16	Maryland	17	10
17	West Virginia	656	337

Appendix J—*Continued*

	District	Tom Lewis	John Walker
18	British Columbia	876	304
19	Tennessee	518	87
20	Alabama	182	282
21	Oklahoma, Texas, Arkansas	1,873	3,490
22	Montana, Wyoming	1,891	976
23	Kentucky	1,707	852
24	Missouri	2,064	852
	Total	78,408 ½	63,063 ½

Source: Compiled from tally sheets in *Proceedings of the Nineteenth Annual Convention of the United Mine Workers of America* (Indianapolis: Hollenbeck, 1910), p. 1064-1152.

Appendix K

WAGES OF UNSKILLED STEELWORKERS, 1901-1920

Year	Hourly Wage	Average Annual Wage
1901	13.7¢	$ 443
1902	14.0	452
1903	14.5	468
1904	14.3	468
1905	13.7	442
1906	14.0	452
1907	14.3	461
1908	15.1	409
1909	15.0	487
1910	15.2	494
1911	16.1	523
1912	16.5	536
1913	17.4	565
1914	18.2	591
1915	18.1	588
1917	25.8	915
1919	46.3	1,500
1920	51.2	1,659

Source: U.S. Commissioner of Labor, *Report on Conditions of Employment in the Iron and Steel Industry* (Washington, D.C.: Government Printing Office, 1911), 3:81; U.S. Department of Labor, Bureau of Labor Statistics, *Bulletin 252* (Washington, D.C.: Government Printing Office, 1924).

Appendix L

VOTE IN PENNSYLVANIA's 302 BITUMINOUS COAL TOWNS, 1874-1920

Year	Republican	Democratic	Other[a]
1874	10,503	9,067	790 (Independent Labor)
			Greenback
1876	15,729	17,514	11,583
1878	15,587	16,656	9,355
1880	29,689	22,600	2,363
1882	30,114	30,120	1,551
1884	30,282	24,286	1,389
1886	24,047	19,396	
1888	23,988	27,299	
1890	28,098	33,488	
			Populist
1892	26,922	23,702	809
1894	26,218	12,026	6,301
1896	19,411	11,943	1,107
1898	24,263	24,910	7,263
			Socialist Party of America
1900	23,110	16,434	548
1902	21,162	14,555	242
1904	25,319	17,182	1,841
1906	26,419	15,198	2,482
1908	34,133	21,694	2,704
1910	28,661	9,472	9,211
			Keystone
			41,234
			Progressive
			29,931
1912	14,505	21,912	7,806
1914	25,889	22,140	4,489
1916	30,126	24,634	3,730
1920	37,988	19,822	188

Source: From Secretary of State of Pennsylvania, *Smull's Legislative Handbook* (Harrisburg: State Printers, 1875-1921).
Note: Nonunion Westmoreland County is not included.
[a]Votes for insignificant third and fourth parties such as the Socialist Labor party and the Prohibition party are not included.

Appendix M

VOTE IN OHIO'S 221 COAL TOWNS, 1874-1920

Year	Republican	Democratic	Other[a]	
1875	19,902	8,895	Greenback	
1876	15,028	18,089	8,082	
1878	17,094	20,348	7,189	
1880	26,196	23,368	1,064	
1882	27,482	25,398	1,098	
1884	29,001	23,705	1,042	
1886	27,604	23,624	2,711	
1888	25,224	24,900	198	
			Populist	
1890	24,409	22,374	1,724	
1892	18,830	17,625	804	
1894	22,616	14,614	9,082	
1896	34,824	31,386	127	
1898	26,828	30,022	8,878	
			Socialist Party of America	
1900	34,222	28,788	1,098	
1902	33,905	22,736	2,112	
1904	28,151	14,738	2,209	
1906	35,624	21,056	1,336	
1908	34,981	31,245	2,997	
1910	32,938	28,829	7,306	
				Progressive
1912	20,218	14,925	7,929	13,735
1914	26,363	31,185	4,907	3,337
1916	21,488	21,895	2,908	
1920	32,888	17,822	488	

Source: From Secretary of State of Ohio, *Ohio Statistics* (Columbus: State Printers, 1874-1920).

[a]Votes for insignificant third and fourth parties such as the Socialist Labor party or the Prohibition party are not included.

Appendix N

VOTE IN 228 ANTHRACITE COAL TOWNS, 1874-1920

Year	Republican	Democrat	Other[a]	
1874	8,956	7,428	Greenback	
1876	6,529	5,702	13,650	
1878	10,419	8,732	15,307	
1880	13,707	12,968	3,074	
1882	9,886	8,190	2,703	
1884	10,882	9,988	2,798	
1886	13,120	14,580	2,273	
1888	20,748	20,208		
1890	18,415	22,878	Populist	
1892	22,311	23,004	571	
1894	14,462	11,019	382	
1896	13,034	12,667	50	
1898	15,442	21,379	12,516	
			Socialist Party of America	
1900	23,110	16,452	548	
				Anti-Machine
1902	11,896	17,133	9,836	2,483
1904	22,554	12,908	1,979	
1906	25,2222	18,982	2,288	
1908	25,961	23,777	1,948	
				Keystone
1910	13,888	8,112	5,917	15,250
				Progressive
1912	7,845	23,300	6,476	27,835
1914	20,247	19,919	1,576	
1916	31,009	25,818	1,957	
1920	38,988	22,717	288	

Statistics compiled from Secretary of State of Pennsylvania, *Smull's Legislative Handbook* (Harrisburg: State Printers, 1875-1921).

[a]Votes for insignificant third and fourth parties such as the Socialist Labor party and the Prohibition party are not included.

Appendix O

VOTE IN SIXTEEN STEEL COMMUNITIES IN PENNSYLVANIA

Year	Republican	Democratic	Other[a]	
			Independent Labor	
1874	2,280	1,886	367	
			Greenback	
1876	3,224	2,907	2,751	
1878	6,035	9,501	2,089	
1880	6,770	2,995	702	
1882	5,112	5,728	832	
1884	6,241	6,512	303	
1886	9,153	6,142	34	
1888	7,710	5,498		
1890	9,716	12,121	Populist	
1892	12,301	10,241	133	
1894	8,542	2,350	616	
1896	13,244	5,932	242	
1898	14,323	9,978	415	
			Socialist Party of America	
1900	14,384	5,587	478	
1902	13,987	5,284	944	
1904	12,309	6,876	2,902	
1906	14,308	7,224	3,107	
1908	16,684	12,762	4,124	
1910	18,018	16,762	4,502	Progressive
1912	8,892	11,133	10,084	13,788
1914	12,243	11,416	4,314	
1916	26,482	17,100	2,782	
1918	24,233	13,144	380	Labor
1920	26,121	15,343	3,933	552

Source: Data compiled from statistics in Secretary of State of Pennsylvania, *Smull's Legislative Handbook, 1917, 1919* (Harrisburg: State Printers, 1875-1921).
Note: The sixteen steel communities are Bethlehem (steel precincts), Braddock, Donora, Duquesne, East Pittsburgh, Homestead, Johnstown City (steel precincts), McKeesport, McKees Rocks, Monessen, Newcastle, North Braddock, Pittsburgh (steel precincts), Steelton, and West Homestead.
[a] Votes for insignificant third and fourth parties such as the Socialist Labor party or the Prohibition party are not included.

Appendix P

STEEL COMMUNITIES CLASSIFIED ACCORDING TO PERCENTAGE IMMIGRANTS AND FIRST-GENERATION AMERICANS

City or Town	Percent Immigrant	Percent First-Generation Americans	Percent Second, Third, or Fourth Generation
Bethlehem	4	11	85
Braddock	35	32	23
Donora	28	41	31
Duquesne	33	38	29
Homestead	39	33	28
McKeesport	51	54	15
McKees Rocks	45	30	25
Monessen	49	32	19
Newcastle	39.8	23.4	36.8
Pittsburgh	42.2	35.9	21.9
Rankin	50	30	20
Steelton[a]	32	14	64
Wilderming	34	39	32

Source: U.S. Department of Commerce, Bureau of the Census, *Population Statistics (1910)* (Washington, D.C.: Government Printing Office, 1913), 3:587-93.
[a]The significant figure here is 14 percent first-generation American, since 90 percent of the immigrants were disenfranchised aliens.

Appendix Q

WAGE RATES IN UNION AND NONUNION COALFIELDS

1910	Pittsburgh District	Westmoreland County, Pennsylvania
Skilled pick miner	95¢/ton	85¢/ton
Loaders	1.172¢/ton	.095¢/ton
Machine Operator	53¢/ton	41¢/ton
Average daily wages		
skilled men	$2.70-2.80/8 hour day	$2.40-2.60/10 hr. day
Unskilled men	$2.49/8 hour day	$1.60-2.00/10 hr. day

Source: Compiled from *United Mine Workers Journal*, November 24, 1910; Francis Freehan to John Mitchell, September 13, 1910, Mitchell Papers, Catholic University.

1912	Hocking Valley of Ohio	West Virginia
Pick mining in rooms	.6785/ton	.30/ton
Loaders	.547/ton	.23/ton
Drivers	.10/ton	.06/ton
Motormen	$2.70/day	$1.95/day
Brakemen	$2.70/day	$1.95/day
Trackmen	$2.70/day	$1.85/day
Trimmers	$2.47/day	$1.95/day
Carpenters	$2.67/day	$2.25/day

Source: From U.S. Bureau of Labor Statistics, *Bulletins* 358 and 601 (Washington, D.C.: Government Printing Office, 1913, 1924).

Appendix R

PRICES IN A COMPANY STORE COMPARED TO THOSE IN AN INDEPENDENT STORE, ESKDALE, WEST VIRGINIA

Item	Company Store	Independent Store
Flour (barrel)	$8.00	$6.40-6.75
Bacon (poung)	.28	.20
Miners oil (gallon)	1.00	.60
Shovel	1.00	.45

Source: From U.S. Senate, Committee on Education and Labor, *Conditions in the Paint Creek Coal Fields of West Virginia* (Washington, D.C.: Government Printing Office, 1913), 3:220.

Bibliographical Essay

A complete description of all the sources I used in writing this book would be very tedious and repeat much of the footnotes. Therefore, in this essay I only discuss a few of the most important primary sources that I consulted. Most of the other works that I used are listed in the complete bibliography, which follows.

My major source of material for descriptions of strikes was the press. I realize that historians must be very careful when using newspapers, which have not always been known for their judiciousness. Still, newspaper reporters often provided the only available eyewitness accounts of strikes, so newspapers are indispensable sources for the study of labor history. I chose the newspapers I used with great care, and once I concluded that a particular daily was reliable, I used it extensively. The *Chicago Tribune* and the *Scranton Times* were of incalculable value. The *Tribune*, with Henry Demarest Lloyd as labor editor, covered the bituminous coal strikes of the 1890s in meticulous detail. The *Times* provided excellent descriptions of the battles that took place in the anthracite region. Other newspapers either ignored these epic strikes or were so antilabor as to be virtually useless.

The *United Mine Workers Journal,* a weekly, was my most valuable source. The *Journal* not only described strikes and analyzed the political attitudes of the leaders of the UMW but published letters from coal miners and union organizers. The latter often provided clues as to what the coal miners were thinking. I also found some very revealing coal miner letters in the John Mitchell Papers at Catholic University in Washington, D.C. Unfortunately similar material is not included in the John Walker Papers (University of Illinois at Urbana), the Duncan McDonald Papers (Illinois Historical Survey at Springfield), the Adolph Germer Papers (Wisconsin State Historical Society), or in the William B. Wilson Papers (Pennsylvania Historical Society).

One of the labor historian's most challenging tasks is to discover what supposedly inarticulate workers had to say about their lives and jobs. I was able to find more of this kind of material than I thought to be available. The *New York World* published some marvelous interviews with steelworkers during February and March 1912. Between 1909 and 1920, *Survey*, a magazine published by the Charity Organization of New York, printed some interesting articles written by John Fitch, who conducted extensive interviews with the steelworkers of the Pittsburgh district. After the steel strike of 1919, David Saposs interviewed several hundred steelworkers. The transcripts of these interviews have been deposited at Wisconsin State Historical Society. More recently, James Axelrod, a member of the Department of Sociology of Berea College (Berea, Kentucky), conducted a series of interviews with retired West Virginia coal miners. This material, taped as late as 1970, proved to be quite enlightening.

Coal miners and steelworkers also spoke to government investigators and congressional committees that tried to discover why strikes erupted into violence. The Senate Committee on Education and Labor held hearings on the Paint Creek strike of 1912-1913 and on the steel strike of 1919. The House Committee on Rules investigated the Westmoreland County coal strike. The massive transcript of the hearings of the Anthracite Coal Strike Commission is also available. Copies of this document have been deposited at the National Archives and at Pennsylvania State University.

My election data were compiled from *Smulls Legislative Handbook* (Pennsylvania), *Ohio Statistics*, and the *Chicago Daily News Almanac* (Illinois and Indiana). Unfortunately the *Chicago Daily News Almanac* stopped publishing precinct election returns in 1896. I was unable to find such data for the 1900-1920 period. Thus I had to use the more imprecise county election returns for Illinois and Indiana. This was particularly disturbing because Illinois was the seat of Socialist power within the United Mine Workers.

Bibliography

MANUSCRIPT COLLECTIONS

James Axelrod. Personal interviews with Retired West Virginia Coal Miners, tape recorded during the spring of 1970. Berea College, Berea, Kentucky.

Commission on Industrial Relations. "Trade Agreements in the Coal Mines." Unpublished report deposited in National Archives, Washington, D.C., 1914.

Eugene Debs Collection. New York University.

Adolph Germer Collection. Wisconsin State Historical Society (Madison).

John W. Hayes Collection. Catholic University of America (Washington, D.D.).

Mary Harris Jones Collection. Catholic University of America (Washington, D.C.).

Michael Koiskik Collection (including "Proceedings of the Anthracite Coal Strike Commission"). Pennsylvania State University (College Town, Pennsylvania).

Duncan McDonald Collection. Illinois State Historical Society (Springfield).

John Mitchell Collection. Catholic University of America (Washington, D.C.).

National Civic Federation Collection. New York Public Library.

George W. Perkins Collection. Columbia University.

David J. Saposs. Personal interviews with Steel Workers, done during the summer of 1920, Wisconsin State Historical Society (Madison).

Socialist Party of America Collection. Duke University (Durham, North Carolina).

John Walker Collection. University of Illinois at Urbana.

William B. Wilson Collection. Pennsylvania HIstorical Society (Philadelphia).

NEWSPAPERS AND PERIODICALS

Athens (Ohio) *Messenger.*
Chicago Daily News Almanac.
Daily Anthracite (Carbondale, Pennsylvania).
Iron City Trades Journal (Pittsburgh).
National Labor Tribune (Pittsburgh).
New York Call.
New York Times.
New York Tribune.
New York World.
Ohio State Journal (Columbus).
Outlook (New York).
Scranton Times.
Survey (New York).
Wheeling Majority (West Virginia).

TRADE PUBLICATIONS

American Iron and Steel Institute. *Monthly Bulletin, 1913-1921.*
_____. *Yearbook, 1912-1924.*
Coal Age.
Coal Trade Journal.
Iron Age.
United States Steel Corporation. "Addresses and Statements by Elbert H. Gary. "Compiled and bound by the New York Public Library. 8 vols., 1927.
_____. Committee of Safety, Relief, Sanitation and Welfare. *Bulletin, 1911-1925.*

LABOR AND SOCIALIST PUBLICATIONS

Amalgamated Association of Iron and Steel Workers. Amalgamated *Journal.*

American Federation of Labor. *American Federationist.*
Appeal to Reason (Girard, Kansas).
Chicago Socialist.
Free Press (Newcastle, Pennsylvania).
Cleveland Citizen.
Galesburg Labor News (Illinois).
Indianapolis Union.
Industrial Worker (Spokane, Washington).
International Socialist Review.
Miners Magazine (Denver).
New York Call.
Party Builder of the Socialist Party.
Quincy (Illinois) *Labor News.*
Social Democrat (Chicago and Milwaukee).
Socialist (Toledo, Ohio).
United Mine Workers Journal.

OFFICIAL CONVENTION PROCEEDINGS

Amalgamated Association of Iron, Steel and Tin Workers. "Proceedings." Microfilm copy at Cornell University, Ithaca, N.Y.

Coal Miners and Operators of Illinois, Indiana, Ohio and Pennsylvania. *Proceedings of the Second Annual Joint Conference.* Pittsburgh: Myers and Shenkle, 1899.

Coal Miners and Operators of the Central Competitive Field. *Proceedings of the Joint Conference held in Mobile, Alabama, February 24, 1916.* Mobile: Charles Anderson, 1916.

Illinois Coal Operators Association and the United Mine Workers of America District 12. *Proceedings of the Joint Conference held at Peoria, Illinois, February 24-March 13, 1902.* Springfield: Joliet Republican Printing Office, 1902.

Socialist Party of America. "Minutes of the National Convention," (1900-1912). Eugene Debs Collection, New York University.

United Mine Workers of America. *Proceedings of the Annual Convention.* 1892-1924. Indianapolis: Hollenbeck, 1893-1924.

_____.*Proceedings of the Joint Conventions of Districts 1, 7, 9, held at Shamokin, Pennsylvania, May 12-15, 1902.* Scranton: Roth, 1902.

_____. District 12. "Proceedings of District Twelve's Convention" (1906-1916). Microfilm copy at Cornell University, Ithaca, N.Y.

GOVERNMENT PUBLICATIONS

Anthracite Board of Conciliation. *Compilation of Grievances, 1906-1916.* 11 vols. Washington, D.C.: Government Printing Office, 1907-1917.

Illinois Bureau of Labor Statistics. *Annual Report. 1885-1925.* Springfield: State Printers, 1886-1926.

Ohio Bureau of Labor Statistics. *Annual Reports, 1885-1925.* Springfield: State Printers, 1886-1926.

Pennsylvania Department of the Interior. *Annual Report, Part III, 1875-1925.* Harrisburg: State Printers, 1876-1926.

Secretary of State of Illinois. *Blue Book of the State of Illinois 1913-1914.* Danville: Illinois Printing Company, 1914.

Secretary of State of Indiana. *Biennial Report, 1892-1924.* Indianapolis: State Printers, 1893-1925.

Secretary of State of Ohio. *Ohio Statistics.* 1890-1924. Columbus: State Printers, 1890-1924.

Secretary of State of Pennsylvania. *Smulls Legislative Handbook, 1877-1924.* Harrisburg: State Printers, 1878-1925.

Secretary of State of West Virginia. *West Virginia Blue Book, 1916-1924.* Charleston: State Printers, 1917-1925.

U.S. Bureau of Labor Statistics. *Bulletin.* Washington, D.C.: Government Printing Office, 1896-1935.

U.S. Coal Commission. *Report.* 4 vols. Washington: D.C.: Government Printing Office, 1925.

U.S. Commissioner of Labor. *Report on the Strike in the Bituminous Coal Field of Westmoreland County, Pennsylvania.* Washington, D.C.: Government Printing Office, 1912.

————. *Report on the Strike at the Bethlehem Steel Works.* Washington, D.C.: Government Printing Office, 1910.

————. *Report on Conditions of Employment in the Iron and Steel Industry.* 4 vols. Washington, D.C.: Government Printing Office, 1911.

————.*Tenth Annual Report: Strikes and Lockouts.* Washington, D.C.: Government Printing Office, 1896.

————. *Nineteenth Annual Report: Wages and Hous of Labor.* Washington, D.C.: Government Printing Office, 1905.

————.*Twenty-first Annual Report: Strikes and Lockouts.* Washington, D.C.: Government Printing Office, 1925.

U.S. Congress. House of Representatives. *Labor Troubles in the Anthracite Region of Pennsylvania, 1887-1888.* Washington, D.C.: Government Printing Office, 1889.

_____. Committee on Investigation of the United States Steel Corporation. *Hearings.* 8 vols. Washington, D.C.: Government Printing Office, 1911-1912.

_____. Committee on the Judiciary. *Investigation of the Employment of Pinkerton Detectives in Connection with Labor Troubles at Homestead, Pennsylvania.* Washington, D.C.: Government Printing Office, 1893.

_____. Committee on Labor. *Investigation of Wages and Working Conditions in the Coal Mining Industry.* 3 vols. Washington, D.C.: Government Printing Office, 1922.

_____. Committee on Rules. *Investigation of the Troubles in the Bituminous Coal field of Westmoreland County, Pennsylvania.* Washington, D.C.: Government Printing Office, 1913.

U.S. Congress. Senate. Committee on Education and Labor. *Conditions in the Paint Creek Coal Fields of West Virginia.* Washington, D.C.: Government Printing Office, 1913.

_____. *Investigation of the Strike in the Steel Industries.* Washington, D.C.: Government Printing Office, 1919.

U.S. Geological Survey. *Mineral Resources in the United States, Part III, Non-Metals Including Coal, 1899-1924.* Washington, D.C.: Government Printing Office, 1900-1925.

U.S. Immigration Commission. *Reports of the Immigration Commission.* 25 vols. Washington, D.C.: Government Printing Office, 1911.

U.S. Industrial Commission. *Report on the Relations and Conditions of Capital and Labor.* 25 vols. Washington, D.C.: Government Printing Office, 1901.

BOOKS AND DISSERTATIONS

Adam, Graham. *The Age of Industrial Violence, 1900-1915.* New York: Columbia University Press, 1966.

Angle, Paul. *Bloody Williamson: A Chapter in the History of American Lawlessness.* New York: Alfred A. Knopf, 1952.

Aurland, Harold W. *From the Molly Maguires to the United Mine Workers.* Philadelphia: Temple University Press, 1971.

Baratz, Morton. *The Union and the Coal Industry.* New Haven: Yale University Press, 1955.

Bernstein, Irving. *The Lean Years: A History of the American Worker, 1920-1933*. Boston: Houghton Mifflin, 1966.

_____. *The Turbulent Years: A History of the American Worker, 1933-1941*. Boston: Houghton Mifflin, 1971.

Bimba, Anthony. *The Molly Maguires*. New York: International Publishers, 1932.

Bloch, Louis. *Labor Agreements in the Coal Industry*. New York: Russell Sage Foundation, 1931.

Bridge, James Howard. *The Inside Story of the Carnegie Steel Company*. New York: The Aldene Book Company, 1903.

Brody, David. *Labor in Crisis: The Steel Strike of 1919*. Philadelphia: J. P. Lippincott Company, 1965.

_____. *The Steel Workers in America. The Non-Union Era*. Cambridge: Harvard University Press, 1960.

Brohl, Wayne. *The Molly Maguires*. Cambridge: Harvard University Press, 1964.

Brophy, John. *A Miner's Life*. Madison: University of Wisconsin Press, 1964.

Bruce, Robert. *1877: Year of Violence*. Indianapolis: Bobbs-Merrill, 1959.

Burgoyne, Arthur. *Homestead*. Pittsburgh: Rawsthrone Printing Company, 1893.

Byington, Margaret F. *Homestead: Households of a Mill Town*. New York: Charities Publications Committee, 1910.

Cary, Lorin Lee. "Adolph Germer: From Labor Agitator to Labor Professional." Ph.D. dissertation, University of Wisconsin, 1968.

Chaplin, Ralph. *Wobbly: The Rough and Tumble Story of an American Radical*. Chicago: University of Chicago Press, 1948.

Cole, G. D. H. *The Second International, 1889-1914*. London: Macmillan, 1956.

Coleman, J. Walker. *Labor Disturbances in Pennsylvania, 1850-1880*. Washington, D.C.: Catholic University Press, 1936.

Coleman, McAlister. *Men and Coal*. New York: Farrars and Rinehart, 1943.

_____. *Eugene V. Debs: A Man Unafraid*. New York: Greenberg Publisher, 1939.

Conley, Phil. *History of the West Virginia Coal Industry*. Charleston, W. Va.: Education Foundations, 1960.

Conlin, Joseph. *Big Bill Haywood and the Radical Union Movement*. Syracuse: Syracuse University Press, 1969.

Cornell, Robert. *The Anthracite Coal Strike of 1902.* Washington, D.C.: Catholic University Press, 1957.

Cotter, Arundel. *The Authentic History of the Carnegie Steel Corporation.* New York: Moody Magazine Book Company, 1916.

Croly, Herbert. *Marcus Alonzo Hanna—His Life and Work.* New York: Macmillan, 1912.

Destler, Chester McArthur. *American Radicalism, 1865-1901.* New London, Conn: Connecticut State College Press, 1946.

Douglas, Paul. *Real Wages in the United States, 1890-1926.* Boston: Houghton Mifflin, 1930.

Dubofsky, Melvyn. *We Shall Be All.* Chicago: Quadrangle Books, 1969.

Eastman, Crystal. *Work Accidents and the Law.* New York: Charities Publication Committee, 1914.

Evans, Chris. *History of the United Mine Workers of America.* Indianapolis: Hollenbeck Company, 1920.

Faulkner, Harold U. *Politics, Reform and Expansion, 1890-1900.* New York: Harper and Row, 1959.

Feuer, Lewis (ed.). *Marx and Engels: Basic Writings on Politics and Philosophy.* Garden City, N.Y.: Anchor Books, 1959.

Fisher, Waldo E., and Bezanson, Anne. *Wage Rates and Working Time in the Bituminous Coal Industry.* Philadelphia: University of Pennsylvania Press, 1932.

Fitch, John A. *The Steel Worker.* New York: Charities Publication Committee, 1910.

Foner, Philip. *A History of the Labor Movement.* 4 vols. New York: International Publishers, 1947-1965.

Foster, William Z. *The Great Steel Strike and Its Lessons.* New York: B. W. Huebsch, 1920.

Garraty, John A. *Right Hand Man: The Life of George W. Perkins.* New York: Harper and Brothers, 1957.

Gay, Peter. *The Dilemma of Democratic Socialism: Eduard Bernstein's Challenge to Marx.* New York: Columbia University Press, 1952.

Ginger, Ray. *The Bending Cross: A Biography of Eugene Victor Debs.* New Brunswick, N.J.: Rutgers University Press, 1949.

Gluck, Elsie. *John Mitchell—Miner: Labor's Bargain with the Gilded Age.* New York: John Day and Company, 1929.

Goodrich, Carter. *The Miner's Freedom.* New York: Workers Education Bureau of America, 1926.

Green, Marguerite. *The National Civic Federation and the American Labor Movement.* Washington, D.C.: Catholic University Press, 1956.

Greene, Victor. *The Slavic Community on Strike: Immigrant Labor in Pennsylvania Anthracite*. Notre Dame, Indiana: Notre Dame University Press, 1968.

Gulick, Charles. *Labor Policy of the United States Steel Corporation*. New York: Longmans Green and Company, 1923.

Hamilton, Walton, and Wright, Helen. *The Case of Bituminous Coal*. New York: Macmillan, 1925.

Harvey, Katherine A. *The Best Dressed Miners: Life and Labor in the Maryland Coal Region, 1835-1910*. Ithaca, N.Y.: Cornell University Press, 1969.

Hinrichs, A. F. The United Mine Workers of America and the Non-Union *Coal Fields*. New York: Longmans Green and Company, 1923.

Hunt, Edward. *What the Coal Commission Found*. Baltimore: Williams and Wilkens Company, 1925.

Interchurch World Movement. *Report on the Steel Strike of 1919*. New York: Harcourt Brace and Howe, 1920.

Jensen, Richard. *The Winning of the Midwest: Social and Political Conflict, 1885-1896*. Chicago: University of Chicago Press, 1971.

Jones, Elliot. *The Anthracite Coal Combination in the United States*. Cambridge: Harvard University Press, 1914.

Jones, Mary Harris. *The Autobiography of Mother Jones*. Chicago: Charles Kerric Company, 1924.

Kipnis, Ira. *The American Socialist Movement, 1897-1912*. New York: Columbia University Press, 1952.

Kleppner, Paul. *A Cross of Culture: A Social Analysis of Midwestern Politics*. New York: Free Press, 1970.

_____. *The Third Electoral System, 1853-92*. Chapel Hill: University of North Carolina Press, 1979.

Korson, George. *Coal Dust on the Fiddle: Songs and Stories of the Bituminous Coal Industry*. Philadelphia: University of Pennsylvania Press, 1943.

_____. *Minstrels of the Mine Patch: Songs and Stories of the Anthracite Coal Industry*. Philadelphia: University of Pennsylvania Press, 1938.

Lambie, Joseph. *From Mine to Market: The Norfolk and Western Railroad*. New York: New York University Press, 1954.

Lane, Winthrop. *Civil War in West Virginia*. New York: B.W. Huebsch Company, 1921.

Laslett, John. *Labor and the Left*. New York: Basic Books, 1970.

Leiserson, William. *Adjusting Immigrant to Industry*. New York: Harper Brothers, 1924.

Lewis, Arthur. *Lament for the Molly Maguires.* New York: Harcourt Brace and World, 1964.

Lloyd, Henry D. *A Strike of Millionaires against Miners.* Springfield, Ill.: Bedford Clarke and Company, 1890.

Luntz, Herman. *People of Coal Town.* New York: Columbia University Press, 1958.

McMurray, Donald. *Coxey's Army.* Seattle: University of Washington Press, 1929.

Mitchell, John. *Organized Labor.* Philadelphia: American Book and Bible House, 1905.

Montgomery, David. *Workers' Control in America.* Cambridge: University Press, 1979.

Mooney, Fred. *Struggle in the Coal Fields: The Autobiography of Fred Mooney.* Morgantown: University of West Virginia Press, 1967.

Morton, Edward Winslow. *A History of the Great Riots.* Philadelphia: National Publishing Company, 1877.

Peterson, Arnold (ed.). *Daniel DeLeon, Social Architect.* New York: Labor News Company, 1941.

Pinkowski, Edward. *John Siney: The Miner's Martyr.* Philadelphia: Sunshine Press, 1963.

Pritchard, Paul. "William B. Wilson: The Evolution of a Central Pennsylvania Mine Union Leader." Ph.D. dissertation, University of Pennsylvania, 1949.

Ramirez, Bruno. *When Workers Fight: The Politics of Industrial Relations during the Progressive Era.* Westport, Conn.: Greenwood Press, 1978.

Rees, Albert. *Real Wages in the United States.* Princeton: Princeton University Press, 1961.

Robinson, Jesse. *The Amalgamated Association of Iron, Steel and Tin Workers.* Baltimore: Johns Hopkins University Press, 1920.

Rochester, Anna. *Labor and Coal.* New York: International Publishers, 1931.

Ross, Malcolm. *Machine Age in the Hills.* New York: Macmillan, 1933.

Roy, Andrew. *A History of the Coal Miners in the United States.* Columbus, Ohio: J. L. Traeger Publishing Company, 1907.

Schlesinger, Arthur, Jr. (ed.). *The Writings and Speeches of Eugene V. Debs.* New York: Hermitage Press, 1948.

Schorske, Carl. *German Social Democracy, 1905-1917: The Development of the Great Schism.* Cambridge: Harvard University Press, 1955.

Shannon, David. *The Socialist Party of America.* Chicago: Quadrangle Books, 1958.

Suffern, Arthur E. *The Coal Miner's Struggle for Industrial Status.* New York: Macmillan, 1926.

_____. *Conciliation and Arbitration in the Coal Industry of America.* Boston: Houghton Mifflin, 1915.

Taft, Phillip. *American Labor Violence, Its Causes, Character and Outcome.* New York: Fred A. Praeger, 1969.

Temin, Peter. *Iron and Steel in Nineteenth Century America.* Cambridge: MIT Press, 1964.

Thernstrom, Stephan. *The Other Bostonians: Poverty and Progress in the Metropolis.* Cambridge: Harvard University Press, 1973.

Thompson, E. P. *The Making of the English Working Class.* New York: Random House, 1963.

Urofsky, Melvin. *Big Steel and the Wilson Administration.* Columbus: Ohio State University Press, 1969.

Walker, Charles. *Steel: Diary of a Furnace Worker.* Boston: Atlantic Monthly Press, 1922.

Warne, Frank Julian. *The Coal Mine Workers.* New York: Longmans Green and Company, 1905.

_____. *The Slavic Invasion and the Mine Workers.* Philadelphia: J. P. Lippincott and Company, 1904.

Weinstein, James. *The Decline of Socialism in America.* New York: Random House, 1969.

_____. *The Corporate Ideal in the Liberal State, 1900-1918.* Boston: Beacon Press, 1968.

White, Charles. "The Socialist Labor Party." Ph.D dissertation, University of Southern California, 1959.

Wolff, Leon. *Lockout: The Story of the Homestead Strike of 1892.* New York: Harper and Row, 1965.

Wilgus, Horace. *A Study of the United States Steel Corporation.* Chicago: Calaghan Company, 1901.

Yearly, Clifton. *Enterprise and Democracy in Schuylkill County, 1820-1875.* Baltimore: Johns Hopkins Univerrsity Press, 1961.

Zaniecki, Floria, and Thomas, William. *The Polish Peasant in Europe and America.* 3 vols. Boston: Gorham Press, 1918.

Zeitlin, Irving. *Marxism: A Re-Examination.* Princeton: D. Van Nostrand Company, 1967.

ARTICLES

Bemis, E. W. "Mine Labor in the Hocking Valley." *Publications of the American Economic Association* 3 (1888):27-42.

Berthoff, Rowland. "The Social Order of the Anthracite Region." *Pennsylvania Magazine of History and Biography* 89 (July 1965): 261-91.

Carter, Charles. "The West Virginia Coal Insurrection." *North American Review* 98 (October 1913):456-69.

Casson, Herbert. "The Romance of Iron and Steel." *Munsey's Magazine* 26 (October 1906):103-34.

David, Henry. "Upheaval at Homestead." In Daniel Aaron (ed.), *America in Crisis,* pp. 133-67. New York: Alfred A. Knopf, 1952.

Doeinger, Peter. "Piece Rate Wage Structure in the Pittsburgh Iron and Steel Industry." *Labor History* 9 (Spring 1968):78-95.

Fallows, Alice K. "A Woman's Visit to the Coal Mines." *Outlook* 27 (December 1902):105-23.

Fitch, John A. "Some Pittsburgh Steel Workers." *Survey,* January 2, 1909, pp. 543-61.

_____. "Wear and Tear of the Twelve Hour Day." *Survey,* March 5, 1921, pp. 713-32.

_____. Labor: The Early Years." *Labor History* 1 (Winter 1960):3-38.
of Political and Social Sciences 33 (January 1909):87-103.

Garland, Hamlin. "Homestead and Its Perilous Trades." *McClure's Magazine* 2 (June 1894):3-20.

Garraty, John. "The United States Steel Corporation versus Organized Labor: The Early Years." *Labor History* 1 (Winter 1960):3-38.

George, J. E. "The Coal Mine Strike of 1897." *Quarterly Journal of Economics* 12 (January 1898):186-202.

Gutman, Herbert. "Reconstruction in Ohio: Negroes in the Hocking Valley." *Labor History* 3 (Winter 1962):243-64.

_____. "Work, Culture and Society in Industrializing America, 1815-1919." *American Historical Review* 78 (June 1973):531-88.

_____. "The Negro and the United Mine Workers." In Julius Jacobson (ed.), *The Negro in the American Labor Movement,* pp. 49-127. New York: Anchor Books, 1968.

Hanna, Marcus Alonzo. "Industrial Conciliation and Arbitration." *Annals of the American Academy of Political and Social Sciences* 11 (December 1902):22-29.

Harris, Sheldon. "Letters from West Virginia: The Management Version of the 1902 Coal Strike." *Labor History* 10 (Spring 1969):100-107.

Hoffmann, Charles. "The Depression of the Nineties." *Journal of Economic History* 16 (June 1956):118-45.

Karr, Carolyn. "A Biography of Henry Hadfield." *West Virginia History* 1 (October 1965):35-58.

Kellogg, Paul. "The McKees Rocks Strike." *Survey* 13 (September 1909): 652-64.

Korman, Gerd. "Americanization at the Factory Gate." *Industrial and Labor Relations Review* 18 (1965):69-98.

Leiserson, William. "Labor Conditions in the Pittsburgh Mine District." *Annals of the American Academy of Political and Social Sciences* 33 (January 1909):21-39.

Lovejoy, Owen. "Child Labor in the Coal Mines." *Annals of the American Academy of Political and Social Sciences* 27 (March 1905):52-67.

Lynch, William. "The West Virginia Coal Strike." *Political Science Quarterly* 29 (1914):626-63.

Millet, Phillipe. "A Trial in a Coal Mine." *Outlook* 89 (December 1908): 98-117.

Novak, David, and Perlman, Richard. "The Structure of Wages in the American Iron and Steel Industry." *Journal of Economic History* 22 (September 1962):334-47.

Smith, Rufus. "Some Phases of the McKees Rocks Strike." *Survey* 23 (October 1909):38-45.

Spahr, Charles B. "The Miners' Strike Impressions in the Field." *Outlook* 27 (December 1902):78-95.

Stewart, Ernest. "The Populist Party in Indiana." *Indiana Magazine of History* 14 (December 1898): 332-67.

Thompson, E. P. "Time Work Discipline and Industrial Capitalism." *Past and Present* 38 (1967):56-97.

Vay de Vay, Luskod. "Inner Life in North America." In Oscar Handlin (ed.), *This Was America*, pp. 398-416. Cambridge: Harvard University Press, 1949.

Vorse, Mary. "Behind the Picket Line." *Outlook* 124 (January 1920): 138-54.

Warne, Frank Julian. "The Anthracite Coal Strike." *Annals of the American Academy of Political and Social Sciences* 14 (January 1901):15-32.

West, Harold. "Civil War in the West Virginia Coal Mines." *Survey* 31 (April 1913):38-49.

Weyl, Walter. "Mine Discipline, and Unionism." *Outlook* 26 (July 1902): 78-98.

Wiebe, Robert. "The Anthracite Coal Strike of 1902: A Record of Confusions." *Mississippi Valley Historical Review* 47 (January 1961): 229-51.

Wieck, Ed. "A Coal Miner's Journal." *Atlantic Monthly* (July 1924):8-23.

Index

AFL. *See* American Federation of Labor

Amalgamated Association of Iron and and Steel Workers (AAISW): destruction of, 18; 1877 strike, 14; 1890s weakening, 102; impotence of, 153; organization of, 14; union contract, 15; worker trust of, 16

American Federation of Labor (AFL): Bill of Grievances, 98; as socialism antidote, 10; and steelworker organization, 113; strike policy, 10

American Iron and Steel Institute, 121

American Political Tradition (Hofstadter), xv

American Sheet and Tin Plate Company, 113

American Socialist party. *See* Socialist party

Anthracite coal industry: and class lines, 66; labor force growth, 35; and labor peace, 34; as monopoly, 34; and railroads, 73; strikes, 39, 47, 62-64, 69, 164 (appendix G); and town elections, 77 (table), 173 (appendix N); wages, 34, 35 (table), 167 (appendix I). *See also* Coal industry

Anthracite Coal Strike Commission, 73-74, 82 n. 76

Berger, Victor, 6-7

Bernstein, Eduard, 5-6

Bethlehem Steel, 113

Bituminous coal industry: miner's real earnings, 163 (appendix F); and overproduction, 24-25; strikes, 47, 164 (appendix G); wages, 26, 162 (appendix E), 165 (appendix H). *See also* Central Competitive Field; Coal industry

Blacklists, 67

Bourgeois class, 3. *See also* Class conflict

British Social Democratic Federation, 6

Cabin Creek strike, 140-44, 146

Capitalism: adaptability of, 5, 85; American, 13; maturing of, 4; resiliency of, 9; and strikebreakers, xvi

Carnegie, Andrew, 131; antiunion campaign, 17-18; and steel competition, 17

Central Competitive Field: coal town elections, 54 (table); defined, 43 n.34; grievance procedures, 93; profits and wages, 25; union victory in, 154. *See also* Bituminous coal industry

About the Author

Michael Nash was born in New York City in 1946. He attended Harpur College (B.A. 1968), Columbia University (M.A. 1969), and SUNY-Binghamton (Ph.D. 1975). He is an archivist at Cornell University's Labor-Management Documentation Center and teaches in the extension division of the New York State School of Industrial and Labor Relations. He has contributed to *Science and Society* and the *American Archivist*.